THE INCARNATE GOD

Also by John V. Taylor

The Primal Vision, 1963
The Go-Between God, 1972
Enough is Enough, 1974
A Matter of Life and Death, 1986
Weep Not For Me, 1986
Kingdom Come, 1989
The Christlike God, 1992
The Easter God, 2003

The Incarnate God

JOHN V. TAYLOR

continuum
LONDON • NEW YORK

Continuum
The Tower Building, 11 York Road, London SE1 7NX
15 East 26th Street, New York, NY 10010

First published in English 2004

British Library Cataloguing in Publication Data
A catalogue record for this book is available from the British Library.

ISBN 0-8264-7127-7

Typeset in Postscript Bembo by Tony Lansbury, Tonbridge, Kent
Printed and bound in Great Britain by MPG Books Ltd, Bodmin, Cornwall

Contents

Foreword

John Taylor's greatest gift was as a communicator. Through his speaking and his writing, he reached out to those within and particularly to those outside the churches, inspiring them with confidence in a God of love who is for all people and for all time. His major works, *The Go-Between God* (1972) and *The Christlike God* (1992), became classics immediately on publication and have remained so ever since. However, perhaps it was through his sermons and occasional papers that John spoke most deeply from his heart, and was able to touch and inspire his hearers in their fragility and vulnerability.

Before he was called to be Bishop of Winchester in 1975, John spent much of his working life with the Church Missionary Society, first as warden of Bishop Tucker College in Uganda, then as its Africa Secretary, and finally as its General Secretary. The CMS newsletters he produced then were masterpieces in their own right, finely written and demonstrating theology in a social context. From these developed another book for which he became famous, *Enough is Enough*, one of the earliest to hold our consumer society up to scrutiny, and offer some alternatives. As Bishop, he made it his business to come alongside people in their daily lives, to reach out to millions through the medium of radio and television, and to communicate the gospel in a cathedral setting by means of music and drama, for which he had both passion and great skill. After his retirement in 1985, John moved with his wife Peggy to Oxford, and continued to write and to speak regularly almost until his death in January 2001.

I was John's editor for all of his major books, and it was an honour for me to be asked by his family to be his literary executor. Peggy passed over to me a large quantity of unpublished sermons, some still in John's very distinctive handwriting, and a number of other occasional papers, poems and articles. From these I selected and put together 32 which were published by Continuum in 2003 as *The Easter God*. The first of its two parts focused on the nature of the God who loves through death into life, and the second on how he works in us to give life to the world. In this second collection these themes are, of course, still present, because these were the golden threads that ran through the whole of John's life and work. His dedication was to this God who loves and holds us through the darkness and brings us into the light beyond, and who reveals new life to us by stripping away what is past and urging us into the future. His commitment was to share the good news of the Kingdom – the here and now of God's working in the world – with all who would listen.

In *The Incarnate God*, the focus is on the action of God in our world by his son, Jesus, from his birth at Bethlehem, through his earthly ministry, his crucifixion, his resurrection, to the new era which these events brought about. I have drawn on a wider selection of material, and have included, as well as sermons, a number of the Rosewindow articles which John as Bishop wrote for the diocesan journal, the *Winchester Churchman*. The title of these monthly articles, or letters, was taken from the rose window of the great hall of the London palace that belonged to the medieval Bishops of Winchester, which can still be seen in a ruined gable among the warehouses near the southern end of London Bridge, and he chose it because a rose window is globe shaped – a window on the world. These letters were most certainly windows on the world, daring his readers to take seriously the social issues with which most of us have to engage in our daily lives. In these letters, and indeed in some of the sermons, John put forward some challenging views on the institutional churches, and also on the nature of the ordained ministry, which are very relevant to a consideration of how God works in our present-day world.

John had a great gift for opening people's eyes, for making them see what was all around them, things they had not been conscious of. He was an intensely spiritual person, deeply aware of the mystery which 'is not the unexplained, but the question that persists beyond all possible explanation'. His preaching and writing vibrate with the musical and poetic imagery which was so much part of him. But his real strength as a theologian was in his engagement with the nitty-gritty of the world, in seeing God in and through the 'little people', the world's poor, those on the fringes and margins, those trying to a good job against all odds in a harsh world. It was for them that God became incarnate, and lived and died and lives again among them. He was fully aware, too, of the cost to those who would see things as he did. 'It is going to be painfully hard to turn around and run counter to all the assumptions and habits of the working world. And it is precisely at this point that we shall either prove or disprove that Jesus is alive. For we claim not only that he makes us see things in a new light, but that he sets us free to do things in a new way. It is easy enough to recite that in the religious environment of our Jerusalem, but it is in the Galilee of politics, commerce and international affairs that we actually put his resurrection to the test.'

Margaret Lydamore
September 2003

PART ONE

Birth

*Close your eyes. For into their guileless gaze
the world will pour its pain, forever heaping
its anger on your heart, and you must bear
the outrage of its wounds and you must bear
the blame. Is it for this that you are here?*

1

In the Beginning

'In the beginning' – that's any good story-teller's opening gambit: 'How did it all start?'

'In the beginning' – the words can still bring a sparkle of expectancy to a child's eyes.

'In the beginning' – is the opening phrase of two poems which are familiar to us from the Bible. Yes, poems. The prologue to St John's Gospel is different in style from the prose that follows. Its repetitions are like those of a song or an incantation:

> In the beginning was the Word
> and the Word was with God
> and the Word was God.
> The same was in the beginning with God.
> Through him all things came into being
> and apart from him not a thing has had its being.
> What came into being in him was life
> and the life was the light of men.
> And the light shines in the darkness,
> and the darkness has not absorbed it.

This style of writing is modelled, of course, on the poem of creation with which the Book of Genesis opens:

> In the beginning God created the heavens and the earth.
> The earth was a formless void,
> with darkness upon the face of the abyss
> and the Spirit of God hovering above the face of the waters.
> And God said, 'Let there be light', and there was light.
> And God saw the light, that it was good.
> And God separated light from darkness.

There are other songs of creation in the Bible, some of them written much earlier than that. Indeed, quite apart from the Bible, there seems to be a universal need to lapse into poetry when trying to describe the origin of existence. The earliest known sample of Old English verse was written by the elderly herdsman, Caedmon, in the seventh century in response, so the legend goes, to a vision in which he was commanded to 'sing the beginning of creation'. Some 70 years later the epic poem *Beowulf* tells of another minstrel who sang to his harp how God made the world a shining plain encircled by the sea, and established sun and moon to light its inhabitants. Some of you may recall also how St Francis in the last year of his life, racked with painful disease and burdened by the misdirection of the movement he had founded, composed and sang his famous 'Canticle of the Sun and All Creatures'.

Don't worry: I'm not going on to Milton and a survey of creation poems. I simply want to ask: Why poetry?

Why do people turn to mythology and the evocative language of song to voice their speculations about the origins of time and space, the birth of this universe, the purpose (if any) of existence? I cannot believe it is merely the language of a pre-rational culture, for they knew perfectly well when they were moving from sober prose into the more complex speech of poetry. Poetry and myth are not anti-logical – they can convey argument or description or explanation. But their inner music of echoes, allusions and double meanings so augments their capacity that they can also carry the weight of what lies beyond explanation, the sense of mystery and wonder.

By mystery I don't mean, as in a detective novel, some feature in the story that has not yet been explained. I am not interested in finding gaps in our scientific knowledge in which to track down the footprints of God. Mystery is not the unexplained but the question that persists beyond all possible explanation. Beyond all the physics of sound and the psychology of aesthetics lies the question: Why do I know that this music confronts me as the truth? That is its mystery, which no new hypothesis can take away, and it fills me with wonder. It's very difficult to put that wonder into words, and the language best fitted to express it is that of poetry, even the poetry of young children.

I mention children's writing because I have recently read an interim account of a study of what it calls the 'spirituality' of randomly selected groups of primary school children in Nottingham and Birmingham. The researchers have yet to come across a child who does not have an inherently spiritual perception of life. They note in particular an intense, though unself-conscious, bodily awareness of the total here and now which is the central component of mystical experience; a spontaneous interest in the fundamental questions of meaning: Where have I come from? What am I meant to do? – and an uninhibited capacity for wonder.

But the researchers are finding that at 10 or 11 years old this dimension of a child's perception is repressed, edged out by the facile and partial explanations of our workaday secularism. The writer instances the young child's delight in the mystery of the flame that appears when a match is struck. The charm of that naive wonder does not deter us from dissipating it with some simplistic reference to chemical reactions. Our itch for rationality is satisfied without plunging into particle physics to reveal that the wood of the matchstick, the card of the box and the fingers that hold them are all composed of the same flaming energy. That is too mysterious for our adult imaginations to live with, so we sell the children short. The author adds: 'They need to understand that scientific explanation is never more than a humanly constructed account of the fundamentally enigmatic nature of physical reality.' Mystery, as I have said, is the question that persists beyond all possible explanation.

So let me end by enumerating those areas of mystery which the two creation poems I quoted earlier set before us for wonder and contemplation.

First there is the absolute mystery of existence itself. The great philosopher of this century, Ludwig Wittgenstein, expressed it memorably: 'Not *how* the world is, is the mystery, but *that* it is.' Beyond all the explanations the question persists: Why should there be anything at all, rather than just nothing?

Then, given the existence of matter, there is the mystery of progressive development. No new ingredient has been added at any point to the primordial matter of which the universe has built itself up. What have occurred all the way along are new ways of organizing what was already there. An original simplicity became more and more complex; homogeneity grew more and more diverse. But why should simple systems tend to develop into complex ones and not in the other direction? Has mere potentiality the power to thrust life forwards in the direction of greater sensitivity, consciousness and freedom?

That question brings us to the mystery of the human spirit – by which I mean the creativity that can both perceive and bring into being the truth that lies beyond the physical properties of music or art, and the capacity to respond to that and every other mystery in the very terms in which we relate to the mystery of another human person: I am – Thou art.

This capacity is what the Genesis poem calls 'the image of God'. 'God created humanity in his own image. In the image of God he created him: male and female he created them.' Because of humanity's unique capacity to recognize and respond to 'the mystery of things', we may all too easily adopt what modern cosmologists call 'the anthropic principle' – seeing ourselves as the Creator's sole interest and presuming upon a very unmysterious familiarity with him. As a corrective, we need to read the longest creation poem in the Bible, Job 38–41, which Tennyson called 'the greatest poem of ancient or modern times'. In verse after resounding verse of stupendous imagery the pageant of creatures, from the dawn and the ocean's bed to the warhorse and the crocodile, is paraded in all its magnificence and fascination – and there isn't a human face amongst the lot. Instead the taunting question is repeated: Where were you? Modern cosmology puts the same question. This is not a man-centred universe.

Getting the relationship wrong is the perennial human sin. But imagining that human sin is the only accident in the story is another form of the same arrogance. Creation's story has been full of accidents, full of flawed relations. It had to be if it was to bring forth freedom and sensitivity and consciousness. But that explanation also only goes so far. Beyond it lies what the Bible calls the 'mystery of iniquity', and that is the risk incurred by the act of creation itself. Even a human creator learns that, as Simone Weil put it, 'Creation is abdication.'

That shocking thought brings us to the mystery of Christ, which is the theme of the second creation poem. The man Jesus was prepared to incur the risk of creating a new kind of community which he called, using a familiar term, God's rule, the Kingdom of God. He called people to follow his lead in living as though God were already in control of society. He paid for it with his life, believing that this would enable the enterprise to triumph. That is as far as our explanation of him as a historical figure can take us. But people of his generation, and of every generation since, have seen beyond all possible explanation the mystery of his person – something more. Here, in the language of a human risk-taker, was the very word of the divine risk-taker – the unfathomable Creator disclosed in human action. 'The Word became flesh and dwelt among us and we beheld his glory.'

2

He Could Not Have Come at a Worse Moment

'He could not have come at a worse moment' is how Mary might have described it in later years. It was one of those calamities that can happen to any of us unless we have enough ready cash to buy ourselves out. The first phase of the new imperial taxation was taking place: that is to say, an exact survey of land property and a systematic inventory of all taxable persons and objects. When a juggernaut bureaucracy fixes a date and orders all citizens to appear in person at the correct registration place it makes no allowance for such personal misfortunes as sickness or the beginning of a woman's labour.

It was not so much that Joseph and Mary were poor, though they qualified for the reduction in the offering that had to be made after the birth of a child. Carols and sermons have made too much of the rustic filth of the stable. When the waiting crowds slept rough in the courtyard of the caravanserai, anyone in Mary's predicament might have found a sheltered spot for the baby in one of the stone feeding-troughs built against the wall. No, they may not have been badly off, but they suffered the kind of blow that can start a family's decline into destitution. From the very beginning of his incarnation the Son of God identified himself with the dreadful vulnerability of the poor.

In doing so he was consistent with the God who had revealed himself to the Jewish people. Theirs was the God who had had regard for the slave labourers in Egypt, noticing the unnoticed, and had championed their cause. The devotees of such a God were to do the same in their own community life. Again and again this is given as the ground for their laws of compassion and justice. 'Remember that you were slaves in Egypt; that is why I command you to do this.'

Throughout their history they were made to experience this continuous vulnerability and victimization in order that they should learn to know God as the one who is on the side of the powerless and wretched

7

and demands that his people also should be so. A church whose clergy regularly recite the Jewish psalms must surely be aware of this. They are the typical songs of the oppressed, mingling the ringing tones of trustful hope, the snarl of revenge, and the whine of self-pity and paranoia. Not always a pleasant voice, but utterly authentic. It is the voice of those with whom God identifies himself even when we find it hard to do so.

'Thou makest us to be rebuked of our neighbours, to be laughed to scorn, and had in derision of them that are round about us.' There speaks the little kingdom, hemmed in by the conflicting imperial powers. But it is the same experience and the same cry as that of the poorest and most helpless citizens of that nation, when exploited by the rich and powerful. 'The poor committeth himself unto thee, for thou art the helper of the friendless. Break thou the power of the ungodly and malicious.' Often it is impossible to tell whether it is the voice of the individual or of the nation that cries out. What is certain is that God is on their side because they are weak.

The poor, as Jesus said, are always with us; but they are not always the same people. As social conditions change, the victims of an earlier decade are given justice and security. But there are always others who through some circumstance beyond their control find it harder to get a job or a house or a loan, and are pushed around by the more fortunate. At present one can readily think of some of the coloured people, single parents, gypsies, the poorly educated, some pensioners, ex-prisoners. No doubt the list could be extended, for the problem lies in the fact that 'the poor' are never noticed soon enough.

But can it be assumed that the church will always be among the first to notice and to champion them? I have come to believe that this is one of the most crucial questions confronting all Christian people today. It ought to be a foregone conclusion that the church takes up the cause of the disadvantaged, whoever they may be, and when we see a Mother Teresa we are proud to recognize the true nature of the church in her. But it is not always so.

During my brief visit to Costa Rica last July, some of us were taken by a government social worker, a fairly unsophisticated but devoted girl, to see a squatters' settlement in the middle of the capital, San José. On the steep muddy banks on both sides of a small, filthy river, 40 families had huddled together their home-made shacks under the shelter of a road bridge. All of them had come in from the country, from 12 to seven years ago, and had been there ever since. Formerly they had managed their own smallholdings or worked as farm labourers; but either crop disease had made them bankrupt or the farms had been bought up by international companies and mechanization had put them out of their jobs. It was one of those calamities that, as I have said, can start a downward skid. Homelessness had driven them into the city, but they had no skills to compete for jobs in a situation of high unemployment. A few got casual work, such as selling newspapers on the streets, but most lived by begging or prostitution.

With desperate resourcefulness they had put together their homes of foraged planks and corrugated iron, propped on long stilts against the slope and linked one with another by duckboards and teetering ladders. Now and then, someone's home toppled into the river, but they could only remember two occasions when children had been drowned, and the fabric was salvaged and nailed together again. Several of them, in fact, had wired tins of growing flowers to the sides of their houses, and although none of them had any right to be there, a despairing local government had given them a cable link to the electric mains and allowed them to run rubber hosepipes from a standing tap. There were no drains, of course, although one family proudly showed me a little outhouse, containing a stoneware lavatory pan, built out like a 'gardy-loo' over the river!

In most of these ramshackle homes there were about eight children, and the parents had been so defeated in the struggle to keep things clean and in some sort of order that the chaos seemed to have entered into themselves. They had lost the ability to manage and co-ordinate, and there was a high incidence of mental breakdown. They had not been like that in the country, one of the men told me. Donna Marguarita, whose common-law husband regularly beat her up, lived in a perpetual high rage. The only thing in her house that looked new and clean was the packet of tranquilizers which, through the help of the young social worker, a doctor regularly prescribed for her. The family was acting out something very diabolic. One of her adult sons raped his three-year-old sister and she had turned him out of the home. An eight-year-old and a four-year-old were out begging on the streets when we called, and already the authorities were trying to get a court order to remove her younger children. She was afraid she would go stark raving mad if they took them away.

Fifty yards away at one end of the bridge under which these homes are clustered there is a church. The mother of the first family we visited is a regular member and knows the priest, who comes to celebrate mass twice a week. But he has never visited the shacks. Although the walls of her hut were covered with religious pictures, it had not occurred to her that he might be a source of help. The social worker had in fact been to see him at his other church. He told her the shack-dwellers were not his responsibility and she must not try to make him feel guilty.

I thought of that again when I was looking at an exhibition of the pictures of L. S. Lowry at Burlington House. His mill towns during the depression are full of churches, their spires and towers mingling with the tall chimneys above the streets full of little people. In some of his paintings a church like a dark triangle occupies the whole space at the end of a road. But their doors are never open. No one goes in or out. They seem to be symbols of a powerful absentee authority.

Not a true picture, I know. But that it should ever have been possible for anyone to doubt that the church of Jesus Christ is the friend and champion of the little people is enough to make Christmas angels weep. We might well spend some quiet period in Advent trying honestly to understand how such ambiguity about the church's position could have come about, and what sort of individual refusals or assumptions have contributed to it. Then perhaps we shall have a new and costly commitment to offer the Child when Christmas comes.

3

What Happened

Returning to the Holy Land this year brought home to me more strongly than ever the 'happened-ness' of the life of Jesus Christ. So much hangs on this that we ought to take the greatest possible care to tell the story and explain what it means to us in ways that do not make it unnecessarily difficult for people of our generation to believe that it actually happened. This does not require us to expurgate the well-known gospel. But if it is indeed the story of the Word made flesh, then we can best tell it by being very down-to-earth. The more we help people to see Jesus as a real man among men, the more they will see God in him. That is how it was in his own day, and that is the only way in which the same faith will be reborn today.

Take the Christmas story, for example. I love the cribs and carols and nativity plays as fondly as anyone. Yet I am afraid that all this lovely embroidery and legend creates a tale which children unerringly put into the same class as Santa Claus and Cinderella, and stop believing in any of them at about the same time. Even those who have to preach on Christmas Day find it quite difficult to remember how little of all this can actually be found in the Gospels, and how much more believable they are.

Does it matter so much? Well, a month ago a child in a Junior School assembly asked me: 'How can your crosses have come from Bethlehem? Bethlehem's up there' – pointing to the sky. And maybe you remember a brilliantly presented television programme some years ago in which the lecturer tried to demonstrate how many incidents found their way into our Gospels because the early church piously transferred prophecies and legends from the Old Testament. Into a Christmas crib he introduced the three traditional magi with the words, 'Gentiles shall come to thy light, and kings to the brightness of thy rising.' It was convincing and disturbing until one remembered that the Gospel does not call them kings. That word, and the idea that there were three of them, and their beautiful sonorous names, all belong to the later embroidery. There is no connection between St Matthew's 'wise men' and Old Testament prophecies.

Let us enjoy the legends, then, as we do the Christmas tree and mistletoe, but let us teach the story in its New Testament simplicity. There was a census (not a taxation, as the Authorized Version says), but whatever was the date when the edict went out from Rome, we know that it took many seasons to complete in the various regions of the empire, so arguments about the 'year of the census' prove nothing. Like everyone else, Joseph and Mary went up to the place of their families' origin and there her child was born. The limestone hills of the Holy Land are honeycombed with caves which even to the present day people have put to good use as water-cisterns, tombs, cellars or additional rooms to their homes. There is a string of six or seven of them under the Church of the Nativity in Bethlehem, and the one which tradition has called the birthplace of Jesus, with its two niches, would have made a capacious storeroom at the back of someone's house. The Aramaic word for a manger can equally well mean a fodder-store, and this is, perhaps, the more likely meaning in this case. It is interesting that most Arabs are greatly offended by the thought of a woman, whatever her difficulties, putting her baby in an animal feeding trough. Nor does the story suggest that the 'manger' belonged to the inn, and it seems more likely that, failing to find room in the public caravanserai, the couple begged shelter from some householder who offered them his cave-store for the night.

Angels occur frequently in the Christmas stories and, if we allow legend to draw our mental pictures of them, they contribute considerably to the fairytale impression. Since I do not know what an angel is, I cannot disbelieve in them. As the Polish poet Czeslaw Milosz delightfully puts it:

> All was taken away from you:
> white dresses, wings, even existence,
> Yet I believe you,
> messengers.
> There where the world is turned
> inside out, a heavy fabric
> embroidered with stars and beasts,
> you stroll, inspecting the
> trustworthy seams.

Angels are visionary experiences accompanying a message or flash of understanding. What 'came upon' the shepherds was 'the angel of the

Lord', which is a phrase in the Old Testament meaning some physical impression of the presence of God himself. It was a light and a voice, as at the conversion of St Paul, and a sense of praise that filled the air. Angels belong to the same category of reality as the voices which brought their message to Joan of Arc, and Bernard Shaw showed deep religious insight when he made her answer the sceptic who insisted that they were only her imagination: 'Of course. That is how God does speak to us.'

It is harder to fit a miraculous conception into a 'down-to-earth' story. For many Christians the virgin birth is a most precious and significant article of faith, and there is no need to abandon it. But one has to admit that on this point the argument about the Old Testament carries some weight. When Isaiah spoke his famous prophecy the word he used meant any young woman, married or unmarried. He was not foretelling a virgin birth, but simply promising King Ahaz how short the time would be before unexpected desolation would befall his two great enemies (Isaiah 7.10–16). But by the time of Jesus people were using a translation of the Old Testament in Greek which changed the passage into a prophecy of a miraculous birth. So, in their excitement at finding how Old Testament promises seemed to have pointed to Jesus, Christian disciples might have drawn the conclusion that this also referred to him and the manner of his birth.

Some find no difficulty in believing that God sometimes suspends the laws of his creation. Others feel that this is somehow out of character and prefer to think that in every 'miracle' some natural factor, though hidden as yet from our knowledge, is called into play. I may be talking biological nonsense, yet I shall not be surprised if our frightening genetic engineers light upon some form of stimulus, other than male insemination, that can activate an ovum to start reproducing its cells – though that won't answer all the questions.

But, however we personally resolve this matter, let us not make it central to the story. Belief in the incarnation never depended on this. If, as we affirm, the fullness of God's being was once contained in One who was his creature and his child like the rest of us, then God was always the kind of God for whom this was natural. It is our myth of a god for whom this is inconceivable that has to go. A Creator whose love is such that he has always known his creation from the inside needs no miracle as a way in. A Father who always deals with our sin by taking it upon himself needs no generations of unsinning to prepare his way into our midst. I say this with undiminished reverence for Our Lady, whose true mystery lies in the nine months and the 30 years of intimate union with the Lord such as all other saints have only guessed at.

Surprisingly, it was not the cave at Bethlehem but the newly excavated foundations around the remains of the synagogue at Capernaum that brought home to me this time the sheer wonder of incarnation. Part of the town of Jesus' day has been uncovered. There is a grid system of narrow alleys, and each rectangular block of dwellings comprises three or four family apartments sharing a central court or workspace. One can readily envisage Simon Peter with his wife and children occupying one group of small rooms, his brother Andrew and his family another, and his mother-in-law a third. The walls are of uneven chunks of black basalt, one storey high, with stairs that must have led to flat roofs of reeds and mud. The rooms are cramped and must have been gloomy, stifling and crowded, especially in the quarter close to the lakeshore, where several fish-hooks have been found.

Here, in what we could only call a slum, where privacy was unknown, Jesus made his home after leaving Nazareth. This was called 'his city', and the men, women and children who spilled out of all those dark homes, streamed down the alleys and crammed the house where he was talking, till it reeked of their toil and poverty and sickness, these were his people. They pressed upon him because he spoke like one of them, and with him there was no need to explain their desperation or their dreams. So long as they could hear that voice and touch that hand they knew God had not foresaken them. Look into their faces rather than the charmed circle around the crib if you want to understand Christmas.

4

The True Image of God

At Christmas time all over the world the eyes of millions of Christians and of thousands who are not Christians are turned towards one point. The birth in the cave-stable has laid hold of human imaginations so that we feel it is not just an attractive incident, but an event which tells a secret and gives us the clue to the meaning of everything: the baby in the manger tells us what God is like and what he is doing with the world.

Personally, I can accept the Christmas stories as the way it actually happened – though I can't pretend I know what the shepherds or Mary herself actually experienced when, as their faraway world put it, they saw angels. But if you feel these stories sound like the legends people weave around the very great ones, then think what this means. Because of what happened just after his death by crucifixion, the friends of Jesus became certain that he, all along, had been the Word of God, the true image of God. And believing that, they wove around his birth these legends of poverty and cold and defencelessness. Not what we would have embroidered about the coming of a Son of God. If these were legends, those who told and retold them clearly believed that the baby in the manger tells us what God is like.

Whichever way you look at it, the birth at Bethlehem and the death on the cross disclose the same secret about God, the same mystery that no logic could have worked out nor imagination guessed. The resurrection did not cancel the truth we see in the cross any more than the omen of a new star in the sky contradicted the helplessness of the new-born child. St Paul summed it up in the first chapter of his first letter to the Corinthians, verse 25: 'The weakness of God is stronger than men.' God's weakness is stronger. God's weakness. That quite extraordinary, almost unthinkable, phrase gives us the secret of Christmas.

Why should God be weak? Why should he need us? Because he who is the infinite and eternal love desired to bring into being something that was not himself, out of which the same love might emerge and respond. So the Everlasting Love set about the enormous adventure of creating an environment in which the other love might grow. It had to be an environment of consciousness and freedom. So from the outset God's hands were tied. For love does not invade the other or take over control. Love needs the other's love but cannot command it. Love is always open to being hurt and defeated. And it is only by pure faith, love's faith in itself, that we dare to affirm that this weakness is stronger than any other power, stronger in the end.

Let your mind dwell upon the scene of Christ's nativity, and you will find there is no need for any controversy between a slow evolution and a divine creation. When this kind of God sets about creating consciousness and freedom in all the persevering weakness of love, it will not be done quickly. This God is present and involved in each part of the process. His strength is the strength of the hills which slowly crumble and bleed their dust to make the fertile soil in which the grass can grow. Take any blade of grass between your fingers and gently stroke its frail silky ribbon. There is such delicate sensitiveness in that green tissue. It has taken millions and millions of years to make. So insignificant and so easily destroyed, yet without its invincible perseverance we and our kind could never survive. Stroke it gently, then, with wondering reverence and you will be very near to worshipping the God of Bethlehem. This God goes the way of every seed that falls into the ground and dies that new life may arise. This God suffers with every tingling nerve and no small bird falls but he falls with it. For the hope that is set before him he endures the cross of all the waste and accident of the long unfolding.

Let your mind dwell upon Bethlehem, and your Christmas festivity can include every bereaved and suffering family in our land. And in every third world country, every country traumatized by war, the only kind of God who makes sense is the one who is never on the side of the big battalions and knows nothing of that sort of power, but can say with literal age-long truth, I was hungry, I was naked, I was in prison. There is no contradiction between this Christmas message and the people's agonized and invincible hope.

Let your mind dwell upon Bethlehem, and the weakness of God will command your worship more than the images of his omnipotence ever did. I recall a wistful Muslim from Pakistan who said: 'I did not want to change my religion. I did not want to join the church. I am a Christian for one reason only. Having seen Christ, I can worship no one else. And if ever someone proved to me that, after all, God is not like what I see in Jesus, I should turn atheist. I had rather kneel down and worship the next little child that offered me its stick of candy out of love.'

5

Strangers with Camels

Epiphany – the shining forth of Christ to the Gentiles, to the wider world beyond the chosen people of the Old Testament, the Old Covenant. This is where you and I come into the gospel story. The Wise Men are our representatives, bringing our history, our world of ideas, our arts and sciences to his light which, ever since, has been shining upon them. This is what we celebrate today.

Yet we have to admit that those astrologers from some oriental court with their foreign speech and their exotic gifts seem incongruous visitors even after all these years. The Judaean shepherds straight from their sheepfold were much more in place. They knew about poverty and were not surprised at an emergency birth in a stable cave and Mary could answer them without shyly hiding her breast. The Word made flesh had come unto his own people and his own people were mostly poor and unlearned. They were the common people who 30 years on heard him gladly when he proclaimed good news to the poor, for he talked like one who understood the daily struggle and was more at ease in their company than in the homes of the great. And it was unimaginably good news that God himself in all his glory has more in common with the uncomplicated, the humble and the generous than with the proud and self-satisfied; that this Christlike God is as open and welcoming as Jesus was to the empty-handed who know their need of him.

But now these mysterious strangers are at the door with their jingling camel train disturbing the night. They come from beyond the small circle of his own people. They are the world that knew him not, though he was in that world and the world was made by him. They not only represent us in our Gentile background but, within the family of nations, represent the wealth, the might and the expertise of the great powers: Rome and Greece to the west, and Parthia and the Indus Valley in the east. Or, to use our own language, the United States, Western Europe, the Soviet

19

Union and Japan. And Palestine in Jesus' day was what we call a 'third world country' – impoverished, exploited, and culturally set at naught. Most of its people, as I have said, were in great poverty, and those who had wealth or power had mostly come by them through corruption. No wonder Jesus exclaimed that it's easier for a camel to get through a needle's eye than for the rich to enter the Kingdom of God.

Yet here they are at the door in Bethlehem, camels and all. Therein lies our hope. The Son of God is most truly at home and at one with his little ones, among whom are not many wise men by the world's standards, not many powerful, not many highly born. But he doesn't reject the rich rulers of the earth or merely make them feel guilty. They too may come to his light and to his love.

But they must travel much further than the shepherds. The road to Bethlehem is not very far to those who have nothing of their own to rely on or distract them. But it is a long hard way to those who have grown used to doing anything they want in the world from their huge resources of tradition, knowledge, wealth and power. They have so much more to leave behind. Yet the journey can be made.

They won't, however, even attempt the journey without a touch of that carefree audacity that is rarely found in the wise men or the great powers of this world. Only the childlike possess it, and Mary's child most of all. And he has no place in his following for the clever ones who would never be so stupid as to chase a wandering star; no place for the men of protocol who know that messiahs belong in palaces and cannot bring themselves to look elsewhere; no place for the affluent who could never dream of setting out at nightfall with treasures for an unknown baby.

Yes, the Gentiles who find the great light are those who come a long way from where they started and are not afraid of making fools of themselves and, finally, are ready to return to their homes by another way, a way that runs clean counter to the plans of King Herod and the rest of the powers that be. I think there is a parallel between St Matthew's story of the magi and St John's story of the coming of the Greeks just before Jesus' death. They too were strangers in the streets of Jerusalem, asking to see Jesus. They too represented the coming of the Gentiles to his light. And his words to them were: 'The hour has come for the Son of Man to be glorified. Unless a grain of wheat falls into the earth and dies, it remains alone; but if it dies it bears a rich harvest. He who loves his life loses it.'

The glory that shines forth to lighten the Gentiles is the radiance of the cross. If we hope to see our nation, our civilization, turn again towards that light then we, who feel the pull of it, must go back by that other way which is the way of the cross – 'a stumbling block to his own people the Jews, and folly to the powerful Gentile nations, but to those who are called, to as many as receive him, the power of God and the wisdom of God'.

PART TWO

Ministry

Now rumour of God's rule is in the air.
He, knowing the Father near
is rash enough to live as if it were
already here.

6

One Man Stood Up

I want to remind you of an old story – the myth of the sculptor who fell in love with the statue he had carved and how the magic of his love brought life into the marble limbs so that she breathed and moved and looked at Pygmalion her creator and loved him in return. As she came to him in all the glow and glory of life could she have known of the marble quarry, of the great block of stone, of the years of toiling and dreaming, hacking and refining and polishing, in the time before she awoke to life? Did she even guess the meaning of the chips of marble on the studio floor, and even so, how much could they have told her?

This is only playing with fantasy, but like so many of the old myths, there is truth in it. For the making of humankind was like that. For a long time we thought we had sprung complete and perfect from the Creator's hand. And so, in a sense, we had, for until that moment when the first man knew himself to be man, there had been no man. But very recently in our history the eye of science has grasped the significance of the marble chips and the evidence in our bodies and those of other creatures, the chemistry, the rocks, the nebulae – and we have begun to understand the infinite patience of God's long dream, the unimaginable endurance of the divine longing which loved us into life. But even now we cannot guess what is the purpose or the power that God has intended to commit into our hands.

But at that point our own story does not follow the myth. We have looked at the sculptor and then looked away. After all the aeons of his loving we have been unable to love him in return. We have taken the gift of life as a matter of course and gone our own sweet way. Our responses to God have been a mere flirtation, casual with no commitment, running back when we felt insecure but otherwise ignoring him. We know that we ought to love him. We believe, sometimes, that life would be happier, with more meaning and order in it, that our relations with other people

25

would be straighter and kinder, our whole world less chaotic and men-acing, if we did love God. But somehow we can't. As if our heart was still stone.

But God is not baffled by stone. Things may seem to have got out of hand, but they haven't got out of his hands – his sculptor's hands. Long ago, through his prophet Ezekiel he made this promise to mankind: 'From all your filthiness and from all your idols I will cleanse you. A new heart also will I give you and a new spirit will I put within you. And I will take away the heart of stone out of your flesh and I will give you a heart of flesh. And I will put my spirit within you … and you shall be my people and I will be your God.'

A fine promise – but how on earth does it come true? For it's got to come true on earth – not in heaven – if it's to be any use to us. 'I will take away the heart of stone and will give you a heart of flesh.' That's Pygmalion again and the magic of a great love. 'I will put my spirit with-in you.' We have no experience of that sort of thing, except in the work of an artist. He puts himself into his work. Did God do that?

There came a day in the long story when one man stood up quietly before his fellows and said, 'The Spirit of the Lord is upon me.' He said to his friends, 'Believe me that I am in my Father and the Father in me.' Thirty-odd years before at Bethlehem the eternal sculptor had put him-self into his work. The Word, the self-expression of God, became flesh. This was a new creation, a new kind of man who was man through and through with a heart that wasn't stone, but flesh warm and responsive and filled with an infinite love. In that perfect life man returned God's love. 'You loved me,' he said, 'before the foundation of the earth.' His meat and drink was to do his Father's will. And when that love led him at last to the bitter end it never swerved or doubted or faltered. 'That the world may know that I love the Father,' he said. 'Arise, let us go hence.' And he went forth alone to the cross and then the world saw how man can love God who loves him. And, just as we have always known, when that man loved God, life was happy with a serene radiant joy that the world had never seen before, life had such meaning and order in it that there was never a false step, never a rush or a muddle. Relations with other people were so straight, so kind, that they were challenged and lifted and transformed by his friendship. Through that one life the chaos and the menace of the world were met and mastered, and in him all the purpose and power which God intended to put into mankind's hands were realized to the full.

Yet even that would be no use to the rest of us if Jesus Christ remained isolated and unrelated, a unique example but forever out of reach. We can't copy him with any hope of success. The person who merely tries to be a Christian might as well try to be an elephant. But the miracle of Pygmalion can be repeated. Just as God put himself into his work in Jesus Christ, so the living Jesus puts himself into us if we will commit ourselves to him. 'In that day,' he says, 'you shall know that I am in my Father and you in me and I in you.' We can be possessed by him – obsessed, our friends will call it – but they will see the happiness, the newness, the purpose and will wonder.

That is what happened to Saul of Tarsus, as preachers are always reminding us. It's worth remembering because it is so typical, in its way, of what happens when a man is touched by the magic of the love of Christ. Obsessed with religion, this one was, but his heart was still stone. He thought he was loving God but really it was only himself. It's terribly easy for religious people to make that mistake, just as it's terribly easy for the unreligious to think they are loving their friends, or humankind perhaps, when really it is only themselves. But when Saul confronted Jesus, really looked at him for the first time – and anyone can do that without seeing him visibly – he realized what he had been doing and to whom he had been doing it. He realized that he was accepted, that he was under orders, for the rest of his life. He stepped down off his pedestal and walked into the arms of the one who had loved him into life, and whom he would love in return for ever. He knew what he was talking about when he wrote years afterwards: 'If any man is in Christ there is a new creation.' First the old creation – man, the masterpiece of God's age-long patience, who finds it impossible to respond deeply enough to the Creator's love. Then the New Man, Jesus, who was God's own self-involvement in humanity and who responded to the Father with a perfect love. And now in the midst of the old creation the new creation which is the people whom Jesus has drawn to himself. Paul of course was a genius. Whatever he did he did, as it were, to a fanfare of trumpets. We are not like that and our lives are pitched in a lower key. So also our confrontation with Jesus, our transformation by Jesus, is likely to be less dramatic, more quiet and mundane. But the old miracle will be in it just the same.

What is the sign by which we can tell whether our commitment to Jesus Christ is real or not? I think one might call it 'outwardness'. Instead of a basically inward look of self-interest, self-esteem, self-sufficiency, the heart is turned outwards. Outwards to God in the first place, looking towards him constantly in love, judging everything by whether it is done in his way or not. Outwards also to other people, actually and quite naturally wanting to do something for them, to be there for them, even if it is only in the simple grace of courtesy. And outwardness that goes on to embrace the world – to be actively concerned with social affairs, with politics, with questions of race and peace because of what these great matters do to people, the people whom our Master loves and for whom he died. For assuredly, when men and women respond to the love of Christ with a total commitment, they find that the whole world is their neighbour, and their will is made one with the love of God to draw the uttermost ends of the earth into the new creation.

7

What Shall I Do With Jesus?

For a brief moment it looks as if summer has come at last. In our gardens the sweet peas are scrambling up their climbing-frames. So are the other kind of peas in our vegetable plots. Looking at one of our plants today I saw the highest of its shoots stretching upwards, like the groping arm of a blind man, halfway across the space towards the next bamboo stick. The plant cannot see or know that there are more sticks above it. It just reaches out in blind hope, its hair-like, corkscrew tendrils ready to clutch at any support as the unkind wind whips the shoot to and fro. I cannot bring the bamboo any nearer. The plant must just go on growing until it finds the next step and can cling to it. I only hope the tired shoot will not droop and let the tendril grasp one of the lower stems, so that the whole plant grows tangled and turned in on itself. As I looked at it, it suddenly seemed to me that that blindly reaching arm was speaking for every human being, crying with the voice of humankind: 'We have struggled for so long; we have climbed so far; but what is it all for? We reach up as if in answer to some promise, some invitation; but is there anything there?' You may think of your individual struggle to achieve something worthwhile in your job, or your marriage, or your personal fulfilment; but is anything worthwhile? Does it actually make any difference in the end whether you go up or down? Or you may think of the human struggle as whole – the infinitely slow development of humankind, the climb out of primitive barbarism to intelligence and civilization. Are we actually going up or down? And if up, what is the point? Do the dreams we dream of a better future have any substance and how can we possibly know? Is there a meaning to it all?

That is almost life's biggest question. It nags at us all, even though we try to run away from it. It is a vital question because, as soon as we begin to doubt that there is any meaning, we start to collapse and fold in upon ourselves and become a tangle. If there is no point to the struggle, no reality in the dream or the promise, no difference between up or down, then our mainspring is snapped, we have no resources, no will, to go on or to care for anyone else. How can we know the answer? How can we become sure? Christians say that they find the answer by trusting the faith of Jesus Christ, trusting what he believed in. He was quite certain that there is something there – something infinitely loving and gentle and suffering and patient. He had such complete trust in it that he called it 'Father', and committed his whole life to do that Father's will. He had every reason to doubt the existence of any such Father when his enemies had him in their hands, and his friends let him down, and no one on earth or in heaven came to his rescue. He even cried to God, 'Why have you forsaken me?' But he never ceased to believe and to trust even when all evidence was against him. 'Father, ' he said at the very end, 'Father, into thy hands I entrust my Spirit.'

That was the most meaningless tragedy, the most embittering let-down in the whole of history. Yet through insisting upon his trust in the God who seemed to have betrayed him, Jesus imposed his own meaning on that meaningless event. It was as though he said: 'This black abyss of despair is going to mean salvation. It is going to be the source of all forgiveness.' It is going to reveal the eternal love of God for humankind. His unbroken faith gave it meaning.

Besides this faith in his Father, Jesus was quite certain that all the dreams of all the little people – their dreams of a kindlier society where-in they would find justice and recognition and hope for their children – would come true, for they were all part of his own much broader, truer dream which he called the Kingdom of God. That dream, he proclaimed, is no illusion; it is so near, in fact, like that bamboo stick, that if you reach up towards it as though you could see it, you will find it.

If only we could trust the things Jesus was so sure about we would be sure of a meaning in life.

But why should we believe Jesus was right?

Because he does not strike anyone as a deluded fool. And because those who have put themselves into his hands have not found themselves to have been deluded.

Napoleon bore testimony to the difference between Jesus and other great men. Near the end of his life he said: 'I have so inspired multitudes that they would die for me. I do indeed possess the secret of this magical power over other men's devotion. But I could never impart it to anyone. Now that I am at St Helena, now that I am alone, who fights or wins for me? But here you see a man who has died still making conquests with an army faithful and entirely devoted to him. His cause goes on. I know men, and I tell you that Jesus is not a mere man.'

No one interested in the meaning of life and its ultimate questions can ignore Jesus. He towers above the giants of history. To some he is an uneasy feeling in times of silence, to others a sunrise of hope in a night of darkness. To all he is a challenge.

I said that 'Is there any meaning?' is almost life's biggest question. There is one bigger question and Pilate was the first to ask it. 'What shall I do with Jesus who is called Christ?' In that question each of us is challenged to a choice and a commitment. We are forced to recognize that it is not for us, after all, to question life's meaning. Life questions us: what meaning are you giving to the circumstances I bring you? Our question cannot be offered in words or arguments or theories. It will be given in action, in our response – our response to Jesus Christ. Trust the unseen Father as Jesus trusted him. And if you find you cannot – and none of us can – then accept the power of Jesus and his living presence to give you his own faith. 'Lord I believe: help thou my unbelief.' Offer him that prayer and in his forgiving, healing love he will kindle his confidence in your heart.

Those who decide to trust the invisible Father as Jesus trusted give their own meaning to their lives. Here is a man who gives meaning to a troubled life by the healing he brings to others. There is a woman who gives meaning to her life through her selfless care of her children. Another woman gives meaning to her childless unmarried life by her service to the unloved, overlooked people in the margin of society. Here is a man who imposes meaning to a life of suffering by the spirit in which he endures it. What have they done with Jesus who is called Christ? They have taken him as the living source of their faith in life and in God. They have made him the power by which they reach up and grasp the dream and the promise. And you can do the same if you will. What will you do with Jesus? That is life's biggest question.

8

Everything Comes By Way of Parables

'You have been let into the secret of the Kingdom of God, but to those outside everything comes by way of parables.' (Mark 4.11)

If you ever listen to Lionel Blue's 'Thought for the Day' on radio, you will know how much his preaching consists of stories, often very funny ones. That is the age-long Jewish method, and Jesus of Nazareth used it too. The argument of the sermon may be beyond your grasp, but a story sticks in your mind, and some time later the significance of it strikes home.

The use of anecdotes, however, runs the risk of your remembering a good story and repeating it to others while completely forgetting where you heard it or what point it was meant to make. And if we read the Gospels carefully it looks very much as though that is what happened to some of the stories Jesus told. Take, for example, what we call the parable of the Lost Sheep. Matthew, in chapter 18, sets it in the context of a discourse about the respect and care which members of the church should have for one another, and the point of the story is: 'Take care never to hold cheap one of these lowly childlike believers – these little people, as Jesus called them – for it is not your Father's will that even one of them should be lost.' Luke, on the other hand, in chapter 15, sets the same story as one of a trilogy in which Jesus rebuts the carping of the Pharisees against his association with undesirables.

Here, then, is an analogy typical of the kind that Jesus liked to use, which had been remembered independently of the occasion on which he had used it and then quoted as part of the teaching of the earliest Christian groups. What meaning would they have given to these unattached stories?

They would naturally look for interpretations which were edifying to Christians, and relevant to the problems which Christians were facing. We do the same. We ask, 'What do these words say to us?', rather than, 'What does the fact that Jesus used these words tell us about him?'

Here is another point. Those early Christian teachers were busy 'searching the scriptures' – the only scriptures they had, which were the books of the Old Testament – and then finding in great excitement how strangely those scriptures seemed to be fulfilled in Jesus and in the church. In doing this they often interpreted the Old Testament as an allegory. The killing of the Passover lamb and, later, the prescribed sacrifices of Jewish worship they saw as allegories of the death of Jesus. The Israelites' passage through the Red Sea and, later, the Jews' return from exile they saw as allegories of his resurrection. So naturally they also treated the parables of Jesus as allegories in which each detail of a story stood for something else. And this inclined them to think of Christian truth, the gospel, as a deliberately hidden message that needed to be decoded – which was a very natural way of thinking once Christians began to lie low under persecution.

What resulted hangs together, by and large, as a consistent developing tradition and there is no need to declare a preference for either Matthew's or Luke's application of the Parable of the Lost Sheep. Both are gospel truths – the value of the fellow Christian, the value of the lost sinner.

And yet there is an immense gain, I believe, and an immense inspiration, in trying to pursue the anecdotes as Jesus told them by lifting the story out of the framework in which the evangelist has placed it, or found it, letting it speak for itself as it stands, free from preconceived interpretation, and guessing, insofar as this is possible, what sort of situation prompted it originally. You may not get any answer to the last question, but what you will find is a recognizable style of approach, almost a tone of voice, betraying an attitude towards people, which is startlingly authentic. It is as though Jesus himself meets you.

A significant number of the parables are not told as stories but presented as an appeal to common experience: 'If such and such happened, how would you react?' Matthew's version of the Lost Sheep begins, 'What do you think? Suppose someone has a hundred sheep …' Luke makes it even more direct: 'Which of you, if he had a hundred sheep …' He invites them to imagine themselves in a certain situation and to say what their natural response would be.

'How does this strike you? A man with two sons asks the first to work that day in the vineyard. He agrees, but doesn't go. The second boy flatly refuses, then changes his mind and goes along. Which is the obedient one?'

Or again: 'What father among you if his son asks for a fish will give him a snake?' A touch of ludicrous exaggeration there – another device in Jesus' armoury.

By this technique of getting his audience to identify themselves with a situation and react to it he left them free to arrive at the true insight by themselves. So a large number of his parables end with a question. He did not impose an answer. The response must come from within themselves if it is to last. But he would often present the situation so skilfully that their spontaneous reaction was the very opposite of the conventional response they would normally have made. Labourers that have done a full day should earn more than part-time workers; but must that bar a generous employer from making it up to the casuals who can't find full-time work? You could have a bad debtor committed to prison until his family paid up; that was the law. But supposing you yourself had just had a huge debt of your own cancelled unconditionally; what then?

Analogies with such a twist in them were calculated to start a disturbing new train of thought. Without realizing it, one's sympathies were running contrary to the conventional wisdom. Without realizing it, one had been hooked. That is the artistry of these parables. Jesus had said, 'Follow me and I will train you to fish for men,' and he was the supreme expert. I believe the evangelist was aware of the symbolism of having Jesus sit in a fishing boat when he first begins to teach in parables. But there are fish that get away. At that point many people, having caught sight of the new truth, drew back, unwilling to accept its implications. And because Jesus had only invited them to imagine a situation they were free to ignore the conclusions they had drawn from it. Jesus had good reason to quote the words of Isaiah: 'You are free to look and look, yet see nothing, and to listen and listen, yet understand nothing. This people have stopped their ears and shut their eyes so that they may not understand with their wits and change their minds and be healed.'

There must have been many occasions when so much fear of the truth, so much deliberate refusal to accept it, must have reduced to despair the men and women who were learning to share the mission of Jesus with him. Especially when the stalwarts of traditional faith were dismissing Jesus' vision of the Kingdom of God as an evil heresy. It must have been at some such moment of hopeless disappointment that Jesus gave them the analogy of the farmer sowing his field. In the long parched summer and the cold dry winter of Israel and Jordan any ploughing before or during the dry season would destroy the humus. So the peasants leave the fields untouched, dry stubble, thistle roots and all, until the rains begin to break. Then they go up and down the entire area sowing in strips, with the plough following, to turn in the seed. What Jesus described was just what always happened, but he made it sound like a chapter of wasted effort. Seed is eaten by the ravenous birds, seed falls where the soil is too shallow above the limestone shelf, seed is overgrown by the tougher thorns and only some of the seed finds fertile soil. It sounds like the familiar gloomy statistics of church attendance – until the surprise ending. The crop that grows to maturity bears so much grain as to exceed all that was sown by 30, 60, even 100 times. Yes, there are failures and disappointments, but they cannot outweigh the increase.

9

The Gospel of the Kingdom

The true meaning of the prayer 'Your Kingdom come' ought to be a subject of supreme importance for all Christians. So I want to spend some time on a simple and direct consideration of the gospel of the Kingdom, and what it means to preach that gospel in our world today.

We must start by looking afresh at the New Testament.

The movement that was led by John the Baptist, and that other parallel movement that has been revealed in the Dead Sea Scrolls, both expressed the enormous excitement of that period over the expected advent of the promised Son of David. Longing for liberation from the harsh rule of the Roman empire, people were looking for the dawn of a new age and the setting up of a new Kingdom. But this was to be different from all previous freedom movements because the initiative was going to be taken by God and he was going to intervene in history. Yet it was in this world that the Kingdom was to be established.

It was commonly believed, in the light of the Old Testament, that the future Kingdom was to be marked by certain promised signs:

There would be a crisis of re-repentance and renewal – not just individual conversions, but a national turning back to God. It would be so deep that it would be like a resurrection of dead men's bones. It would be just as though God had made a new covenant with his people, replacing the old covenant which they had so freqently broken.

Instead of learning about God from their religious teachers people would have a direct, unclouded knowledge of him. This continuous, personal experience of his presence would inspire in them a general obedience to his will and his way.

In place of the hunger and poverty of so many downtrodden folk, caused by the greed and injustice of the few, there would be an era of plenty and of sharing. People thought this would be inaugurated by a great symbolic banquet provided by the Messiah himself.

There would be a general remission of debts and forgiveness of sins such as there used to be on the Day of Jubilee under the old law of Moses.

There was to be victory over disease and every evil power, and the demons would lose their hold over human lives.

Some believed that at this time the Gentiles would recognize the truth of the Jewish faith and would be gathered into the same covenant with God, and then the Spirit of God would be poured out on all flesh.

But before these blessings of the Kingdom could come, there was bound to be a final outbreak of evil which would test the faith of God's people, but which had to be endured, even if it meant martyrdom.

This was the gospel of the Kingdom which was preached by the Baptist, and by Jesus with him in those early days when he was baptizing people in Judaea. Even after John was imprisoned and Jesus had transferred the main arena of his preaching to Galilee, his message continued to strike the same note of urgent expectancy: 'The time is fulfilled and the Kingdom of God is at hand: repent and believe in the good news' (Mark 1.15). Unless the gospel we preach today bears a recognizable resemblance to that, we cannot honestly claim that we are preaching the gospel of Jesus Christ.

Nor can we pray the Lord's Prayer as he intended we should unless we understand how closely it reflects all the expectations of the coming Kingdom which I have set out above. The crisis of corporate repentance – 'Hallowed be thy name.' The direct, unclouded knowledge of God, inspiring obedience to his will and way – 'Abba, Father, thy Kingdom come, thy will be done.' The Messiah's banquet which will usher in an era of justice, liberation and plenty – 'Give us today our daily bread' (or, the bread of tomorrow, the new day). The remission of debts and forgiveness of sins – 'Forgive us our debts, our trespasses, as we forgive those who sin against us.' Victory over disease and demoniac power – 'Deliver us from evil.' The final testing outbreak of evil – 'Lead us not into temptation, do not bring us to the trial.'

But the Gospels make it quite clear that, as Jesus moved into greater independence of John the Baptist, his proclamation of the Kingdom changed key. Both his friends and his enemies drew attention to the change. The emphasis shifted from repentance to the direct, unclouded knowledge of God which is the second of those signs of the Kingdom I have mentioned above. I think this was due to Jesus' own supreme experience of that direct and unclouded knowledge of the Father, and his recognition that other people did not seem to enjoy the same awareness of being God's child.

A second factor which caused this change of emphasis was the power of healing which Jesus had begun to exercise, and which apparently John the Baptist had not exercised. Both his inner relationship with God and his outward manifestation of authority over evil focused the preaching of the future Kingdom upon the person of Jesus himself. 'If I by the finger of God drive out the demons, know for sure that the Kingdom of God has already come upon you' (Luke 11.20). From now on the Kingdom is to be seen in Jesus. Because he is here the Kingdom has already come.

Because of his own inner experience of God, the first of the innovations that Jesus introduced into his teaching about the Kingdom was to see it as an open Kingdom, a Kingdom of grace. It was self-righteousness more than moral inadequacy that would disqualify people from entering this Kingdom when it came. So it belonged most naturally to the poor and the persecuted. The readiness of Jesus to die with the outsiders in society arose from his belief that they would have access to the future Kingdom before the complacent and the censorious.

The only condition for entering into this Kingdom was a person's believing response to its arrival. So if the Kingdom is open, its proclamation must be without compulsion. If all is of grace, all must be by invitation and free choice. I think this is why Jesus invented the parable as his particular method of preaching. A parable does not convince people by arguing; it simply offers the truth to their imagination as a gift to be taken by those who have ears to hear and ignored by those who have not. But this easy-going, take-it-or-leave-it preaching lays a very stern judgement upon us all. If we get the point and respond, the Kingdom is opened to us; if it leaves us cold, we remain outside.

The second innovation which Jesus brought to his preaching of the Kingdom was to call men and women to live the life of the Kingdom here and now in anticipation of its arrival. Since God himself is coming to meet us and is already so near, we must be like him and reflect his nature in all our relationships. 'Be merciful, as your Heavenly Father is merciful.' 'Be complete, as your Heavenly Father is complete.' 'Love your enemies, and pray for them that persecute you, that you may be sons of your Father who is in Heaven.'

In a competitive world the children of the Kingdom of God live to make other people greater than they are themselves. In a world where people keep themselves to themselves and regard their own homes as a private possession, the children of the Kingdom of God open their doors to the most unlikely guests, and are ready to lend what they have or to borrow from others with an extraordinary freedom. In a world of suspi-

cion and heavy armour, the children of the Kingdom of God go on trusting their neighbours and are deliberately vulnerable.

The gospel is the good news of a new creation projected into the old
creation, the power of the future transfiguring the present world. It is the
demonstration of the Father's will and the Father's rule on earth as in
heaven. It makes an impossible demand of us with the promise that the
impossible can be done.

There is a further very important point to be noted. While Jesus proclaimed this rule of God there is no doubt that he saw himself as having
a special role to fulfil in bringing about this enormous change in the relation of human beings to God and to one another. He was the one in
whom the Kingdom was already being realized. His victories over disease
and evil spirits were evidence that the rule of God was at hand. He was
the cause of an overwhelming excitement because people saw in him a
new kind of relationship to God.

And what Jesus was, he called others to be. He summoned the Twelve,
and all others who were ready to trust him, 'that they might be with him'
in living the life of the Kingdom and in knowing God as their 'Abba',
with the same intimacy as he himself enjoyed.

But all this sunshine brought its own shadow. Very early in his ministry
Jesus had to come to terms with the resistance and hardness of heart with
which his preaching was met. People in power, people supported by tradition, and people who were insecure and envious, were not going to be
changed cheaply. And so, while he must have thought of himself as in some
sense the messiah or annointed king who had been promised in the Old
Testament, in his own mind Jesus identified that mythical figure with the
suffering Servant described in the prophecies of Isaiah: 'The chastisement
he bore is health for us, and by his scourging we are healed.' The idea that
the Kingdom of the future is to be inaugurated by the suffering and death
of God's faithful servant is summed up in the special title which Jesus
seems to have chosen for himself, the Son of Man. The phrase is best
translated 'that Son of Man', referring back to the earlier use of the title
in the vision of Daniel, where 'one like a Son of Man' is presented before
the Ancient of Days as an image representing not a single individual but
God's loyal people, vindicated in the heavenly Kingdom after much
tribulation. The 'Son of Man', therefore, means the agent and inaugura-
tor of the coming Kingdom who will enable others to share with him his
special relationship with God through a voluntary acceptance of death.

We must never forget that when Jesus chose the title of 'Son of Man'
he was using a figure with a plural meaning. He called others to be with

him in living the life of the Kingdom, with him also in dying the necessary death for the Kingdom. There are indications in the Gospels that
Jesus expected, almost to the end, that in doing what had to be done to
enable people to trust themselves to the coming Kingdom and let it
transform them, he would not be alone. It had been his confident hope
that those who chose to walk with him would literally take up their
crosses and follow him through sacrificial death into resurrection on
behalf of the world. The Twelve were selected by Jesus as representatives
of the tribes of Israel in order to constitute the faithful Remnant in its
final manifestation as the suffering and dying Servant.

As it became clear to him that the Twelve were not ready to go
through with it, Jesus seems to have set his hopes upon the Three. To
prepare them for what was to come, he had involved those three with
himself in the awakening of the little girl from the sleep of death – an
Old Testament image of resurrection. He had called them up the mountain to witness in his tranfiguration a preview of resurrection. Finally,
when he took them with him into Gethsemane, he clung, I believe, to
the possibility that they would at that time drink the cup that he had to
drink and be baptized with his baptism. The early church realized that
although, in the event, Jesus had had to go forward and make the sacrifice
entirely on his own, the invitation to them to share this with him was
renewed by the Risen Christ, and this became the main significance of
baptism in that early church. 'If we have become incorporate with him
in a death like his, we shall also be one with him in a resurrection like
his' (Romans 6.5). And the sharing of the broken bread and the poured-
out wine was the symbol he gave them to show that they were still
included in his own vocation to be the Son of Man.

His mandate to us still stands: to proclaim the arrival of the future
Kingdom and the nearness of the Father; to live the life of that future
Kingdom here and now; and to share in the dying and rising which alone
unlocks the Kingdom for others to enter in.

When the church begins to share with Jesus in being the Son of Man
it will expose itself to the same humiliation and derision. For striving to
save others from exploitation the church will itself be persecuted. For
opening prison doors and setting people free the church will lose its freedom. For living the lifestyle of the Kingdom the church will be condemned to death. This is actually happening in parts of the world that
seem remote from us. We ourselves do not very often see either a church
that unlocks the Kingdom for others or a church that is crucified. Yet
those two aims, which are one aim, should be always be before our eyes.

I have tried to rediscover the heart of the Christian gospel by asking what it was that Jesus actually preached in the days of his ministry. I have tried to show why his message about the Kingdom of God had to include the sacrifice of his own life on the cross, and his call to those who would follow him to share that sacrifice in order that the Kingdom might be unlocked for all people. But, so that we may see the gospel in all its fullness, we must now try to understand the great change that was wrought upon the disciples' understanding of Jesus' gospel by his resurrection.

Up until then the promised Kingdom was still something veiled in the future. But now, in the raising of Jesus from the dead, God has demonstrated the presence and the power of his Kingdom. Henceforth the proclamation of the Good News must include the proclamation of the death and rising again of Christ. His resurrection, though for the time being it remains an isolated and unique event, is evidence that a new mode of existence, and a new age, has broken into the closed circle of time and space. Something out of the future has invaded the present. The past no longer dictates the limits of what is possible. What the gospel of the Kingdom offers humankind in our day, and what we are charged to preach, is an alternative life-view and an alternative lifestyle. These alternatives are so radical as to introduce a new dimension altogether.

We have to reassure people, and demonstrate it by the way we ourselves are living, that the true fulfilment of the life of our world and of the history of humanity is being given out of the future. It is not being developed out of the past or present. The chain of cause and effect does not stretch ahead to the end; that is the impression we live with, but it is an optical illusion.

This is very important, isn't it, for an age which lives in the unspoken dread of a nuclear catastrophe? When people despairingly assume that the blind pride and selfishness of today's policies are already making another world war inevitable, it really is something to be able to affirm confidently that we are living in a world in which nothing is inevitable. However many mistakes have been made, we can always stop, repent and change direction, because the future is not being created entirely out of the past but can also be given out of the future in response to our faith. The fulfilment of our hopes for this world and for the human race is not going to be made by us or marred by us; it is being given by God. It is his Kingdom which is even now coming to meet us.

Again, we have to proclaim that the Kingdom of God is the fulfilment of the life of this world. It is neither the spiritualized heaven of the hymns nor the idealized utopia of political visionaries. It is, like the resurrection of Jesus, a new creation transfiguring the things of this world. The resurrection of Jesus did not undo the incarnation.

So, although the coming Kingdom will arrive from beyond, it will belong to this world through and through. It is the Father's will and the Father's rule, on earth as in heaven. Because we believe in the resurrection, we should continually deny and defy all such statements as: 'You can't change human nature,' or, 'You must learn to accept the way things are.' Faith in the Kingdom of God lends substance and force to the dreams that we dream, for when people dream with faith in the resurrection their dreams have a habit of coming true.

Because we are so sure of the reality of the Father and the certainty that his rule will come on earth in the end, we are committed to bringing into being the foretastes of his Kingdom – justice, liberation, healing, forgiveness, alleviation of hunger – because it is through seeing these things that other people may dare to believe that the Kingdom is on the way. If we think these foretastes are unimportant we may manage to avoid the cross, but we shall certainly miss the Kingdom.

For those who know they are the citizens of that Kingdom commit themselves gladly and eagerly to the pattern of cross-and-resurrection. They know that this is the way the Kingdom comes.

Something has to be voluntarily surrendered to death in order that the new thing which God wants to give can be brought to life. This does not allow us to romanticize suffering and death or morbidly to seek it for ourselves. But if, by insisting on living the life of the Kingdom in this world, we incur the same hostility as Jesus did, we shall not turn back from the cross, because we accept his formula of life-through-death. The church which lives for itself will always cling to things as they are and be afraid of change, while the church which serves not itself but the Kingdom will be undismayed when some of those things die away because it knows that through that death something else will come to life. When that church sees the kingdoms of this world become the Kingdom of our God, her joy will be so great that she will forget even the scars that she shares with him.

10

The Free Man

*'You did not choose me, no, I chose you, and I commissioned you
to go out and bear fruit, fruit that will last.' (John 15.16)*

I can still remember the first time I walked around an American super-
market in the 1960s. It wasn't simply a question of plain biscuits or
chocolate coated. There were 17 different kinds of ginger biscuit. There
was braised steak with onions, braised steak with mushrooms, braised
steak Mexican style, braised steak prairie style, braised steak Kosher. My
guide pointed out several people returning to the car park with empty
shopping baskets, paralysed by overchoice.

And don't we all waste a vast amount of energy and time weighing up
pros and cons, trying to make up our minds, tormented by the fear that
we made a wrong decision in the past, wondering which would be the
best way to take in the future, looking for signs and pointers, praying for
guidance, struggling to resist the sights that dazzle and the tempting
sounds. Do you really think that our heavenly Father intends us to live in
such a state of anxiety in this maze of innumerable choices and endless
possibilities? All through history the people who got things done for
God and for humanity were those who had no choice because for them
there was only one possibility. The true freedom is that which can say,
'I can no other; I know what I must do.'

We imagine that perfect freedom consists of having the right to choose
what we like from a limitless range of possibilities, but we are the victims
of a great deception, in fact the original lie, the lie of the serpent in the
garden that undermined the true relationship of the man and the woman
with their Creator. 'God knows in fact that on the day when you eat of
the fruit of the tree your eyes will be opened and you will be like gods,
knowing good and evil.' Humanity in its true relationship, its original
relationship with God, knows only God and knows everything else only
in God and God in everything else. There are no alternatives, only the
absolute simplicity of God and a joyful response to him. But without
realizing what we were doing, we have all substituted the knowledge of

good and evil for the knowledge of God. We have learned to see every step and every action as a choice between good or bad, right or wrong. We imagine many possibilities and we set ourselves up as the judges. We enthrone our human conscience as the arbiter between better or worse. Our shame or shamelessness, our guilt or self-esteem, our comfortable or uncomfortable feelings, have taken the place of our simple awareness of God.

The lie that has led us so far astray lay in one word, or rather in one letter − you might call it 'the serpent's hiss', for the lie consisted of the plural 's'. 'You will be like gods.' But there is no real plural to the name God. There is only one. We are meant to know only God and all things in God. We are meant to respond moment by moment to our Father alone. We find it difficult, we find it impossible. We think it is a narrowing, but knowing God alone is not a narrowing down, not a limitation. For God is the infinite ocean of beauty and truth and goodness, and to know him alone and all things only in him is a continual going out and out on new discoveries, right through eternity. But instead we say, which God should I respond to in this decision? Shall I do most good by making money, or by gaining more influence? Shall I follow the way of philanthropy, or should I lay what is most precious to me on the altar? In other words, shall I on this occasion pay my devotion to Mammon, or Zeus, or Eros, or Moloch? Of course we don't put it like that. We think, 'I wonder which way God would prefer on this occasion', as though God himself faces a choice between an infinite number of possible courses of action. God never has to choose. God never, even in imagination, sees many possibilities. Therein lies his freedom. God has no choice. God wills no choice but to do that which perfectly reflects his nature.

Does this begin to sound too complicated? Or rather, is God actually so simple, so undivided, that we over-complicated people cannot grasp it? Then let Jesus be the means by which we see it clearly. In the Gospels, do we ever find Jesus weighing up the various possibilities and wondering which was better and which was worse? That's exactly what they invited him to do with the questions about divorce or the paying of taxes. But they couldn't get him to think in those terms. The knowledge of good and evil, with its innumerable dilemmas, was not for him. He knew only God and everything in God and God in all. And for him to live was to respond joyfully to that God and to do whatever at that moment perfectly reflected his Father's nature. 'I tell you most solemnly, the Son can do nothing on his own account. He can only do what he sees the Father doing, and whatever the Father does, the Son does too.'

For him, to know the Father was to know the Father's will and respond to it as a flower opening to the sun. And there was no way of knowing the Father's will, not from law books, not from other teachers, but only intuitively and unerringly as a consequence of knowing the Father. For the will of God cannot be codified as a general rule applicable at all times and in all cases. The Father's will is always the one thing that perfectly reflects his nature in a particular situation.

So we see Jesus turning his back upon the knowledge of good and evil and the paralysing choices between a score of possibilities, and thus winning back for us all the true relationship between humanity and God in the simple knowledge of his Father and his Father's will. At every point there was but one thing for him to do and he could do no other. He was the totally free man. And he offers that freedom and that simple relationship to us. 'No one knows the Father except his Son and whoever else the Son reveals him to.' 'If the Son makes you free, you will be free indeed.'

11

Not Less Than Everything

'Whoever comes to me and does not hate father and mother ...
cannot be my disciple. None of you can become my disciple if
you do not give up all your possessions.' (Luke 14.26, 33)

Treating your own family as though you hated them, giving up all that
belongs to you, following Jesus all the way to crucifixion – this is one of
those relentless passages in the words of Jesus which sound so extreme
that either we don't even try to relate them to our own experiences, or
we exclaim with St Teresa of Avila, 'Lord, no wonder you have so few
friends when you treat them like this!'

To understand these hard words of Jesus we should remember when
they were spoken. Luke has arranged the middle section of his Gospel
as if everything that happened after the Transfiguration took place during one last roundabout journey up to Jerusalem. There were probably
several visits to the capital during that time, but Luke is saying that, as far
as Jesus was concerned, there was now only one journey's end.

But those large crowds who, says Luke, were travelling with him on
this occasion, had no idea of what lay ahead. They were on their way to
the temple for the festival, and some of the excitable Galileans may have
been hoping that Jesus was on his way to confront and overthrow the
Roman power. It was to them Jesus turned around with the warning:
'First sit down and estimate the cost.'

When Jesus advised people to sit down and count the cost, the question he wanted them to face was not 'How much have I got?' but 'How
much am I prepared to lose?' He knew that great achievements and de-
cisive victories are often gained, not by those with most resources, but by
those who, having weighed the odds, are committed at whatever cost.
The king going to wage war against another king was, as some in that
crowd were hoping, Jesus himself, though the enemy was not Rome but
the powers of darkness. He had counted the cost and knew that his one
supreme resource, which that enemy could never match, was his will to
give up all that he possessed, even life itself. That's what the powers of
evil can never even imagine doing and that must be the means on which

all who follow Jesus in this war must rely. 'None of you can become my disciples if you do not give up all that is yours.'

Yet there is another reason for this total demand that Jesus makes on his followers. He does so because it is you yourself that he has always known and loved, you yourself that he calls. You and I don't know that self yet, not as he knows us. We constantly confuse what we are with what we have. But your bank statement, even if it is in the red, cannot disclose what you are worth to those who love you or to God. Your intelligence and abilities, even if you should lose your memory, are not what the poet Yeats called 'the pilgrim soul of you'. The work you do, the things you achieve, whether small or great, are, like your reputation, your health, your experiences, things that are yours, which may be helpful while you have them, and for which you must be a responsible steward; but they are not you, and can never be a substitute for the offer of yourself, pure and simple, to Jesus Christ.

So in the Gospels you don't find him saying to anyone: 'Follow me and bring your belongings and your gifts with you; we can use them', for that would have confirmed us in our confusing who we are with what we have. No; he said, 'None of you can become a disciple of mine if you do not give up all that belongs to you.' What is more, the word Jesus uses there for 'give up' means literally to separate yourself from – 'unless you separate yourself from all that is yours'.

That word of separation is the one used by the person who once said to Jesus, 'I will follow you sir; but let me first say goodbye to my people at home, make myself separate, distinct from them.' Rightly counting the cost, that man understood that home and family, however near and dear, are part of what is yours, they are not yourself. And you yourself alone are called, you alone can commit yourself to the way Jesus has chosen. But Jesus himself had known in his own experience the necessity of this separation, and so could recognize, perhaps, that this young man was not ready to make it, and that a family gathering and goodbye party could only make it harder for him to do so. So he said in effect: 'If you mean to follow me, come on and don't look back.'

Those who cannot understand such a choice will revile it as fanatical, as an act of hatred towards kith and kin. That is a part of the price we may have to pay for that total commitment which T. S. Eliot described as:

A condition of complete simplicity
(Costing not less than everything)

Does this sound too individualist, as though I had forgotten that 'no man is an island'? Am I exaggerating the literal sense of this word of separation, and ignoring our call to be the one body of Christ? I don't think so. For just as I had to be made separate from my mother through birth in order to become a responsible member of humanity, so, if I am drawn to share the responsibility of Jesus, which is what following him means, I must come to him, naked and unattached through the separations he called a second birth.

But, of course, a birth is only a beginning. Separation has made us ready for a new integration.

Do you know what distinguishes a truly great orchestra from the merely good? They are rehearsed section by section, the strings on their own, the brass separately, and so on. Any wrong balance or false note, even from one player, can thus be identified and corrected, instead of remaining submerged and discordant when the full orchestra plays together. 'Come to me,' says Jesus, 'solo and unaccompanied, and I will blend you to the harmony of my new humanity.'

12

Be Transformed

*'Don't take the fashion of this age as your pattern, but be transfigured
through the remaking of your minds.' (Romans 12.2)*

In the Greek of the New Testament, the word *metamorphosis* is found only
four times. Twice it is used to describe the transfiguration of Jesus Christ,
twice it describes the transfiguration of Christians. What happened to
him is meant to happen to us. 'In their presence,' says St Mark's Gospel,
'he was transfigured'. His clothes became dazzling white with a whiteness
no bleacher on earth could achieve. 'His face,' says St Matthew's Gospel,
'shone like the sun.' It was as if his whole surface appearance became trans-
parent, so that the inner glory of his perfected manhood could shine through.

Many years ago a religious of CSMV wrote this about Jesus' transfiguration:

> We see what would have happened. We see the ultimate perfection
> that God intends for man. No physical deterioration, no rending of
> the earthly body from the soul, but metamorphosis as smooth as
> sunrise into the full-grown man. This is what Adam's uphill journey
> would have led him to if he had stood the rigours of the way.
> Thither the second Adam's uphill journey actually did lead him, and
> perfected man stood on an earthly mountain top and was seen by
> the mortal eyes of Peter, James and John.

He had called Peter, James and John to climb the mountain with him,
not just to see his glory, but to catch a glimpse of what they too might
become if only they could dare to obey the Father as he obeyed and keep
their souls' gaze fixed upon himself alone, until their faces began to reflect
the light that shone from his, 'for we all', as St Paul puts it, 'our faces
unveiled and reflecting as a mirror the glory of the Lord, are transfigured'
– this is the fourth instance of that word – 'are transfigured into the same
likeness from glory to glory. Such is the influence of the Lord who is Spirit.'

This transfiguring of human beings by the transfigured Christ is not
the end of God's creative purpose, for through a transfigured human

community, the physical world in its entirety is destined to reflect the radiance of its creator. St Paul makes the breathtaking claim that the universe itself is to be freed from the shackles of mortality and enter upon the liberty and splendour of the children of God. 'See,' says the transfigured One, 'I am making all things new.'

But by what means can this stupendous miracle be brought about? How, as a start at least, can I or you begin to become transfigured? 'Through the remaking of your minds,' says St Paul. The re-creation of the universe, the metamorphosis of a human being, begins with the refashioning of a mind. 'Let this mind be in you, which was also in Christ Jesus.' And that is a total change of direction, a going against the tide of the fashion of this age. Notice carefully the context into which Matthew, Mark and Luke set the transfiguration of Jesus. It had an essential prelude which they are at pains to point out took place in the previous week. At Caesarea Philippi, Jesus for the first time mentions the cross. Immediately Peter, who had just confessed him to be the messiah, rebukes him, rejecting the very thought of a defeated Christ. And Jesus says, 'Away with you, Satan. You think as human people think, not as God thinks.' 'Don't take the fashion of this age as your pattern but be transfigured through the remaking of your minds.'

The fashion of this age is not obviously wicked and corrupt. It is insidious because it is so ordinary. It consists of attitudes and reactions we all take for granted. It is the climate to which we have grown accustomed. It is a reversal of the fashion of this age when the mind knows, as Jesus knew in that previous week at Caesarea Philippi, that whoever care for their own safety are lost, but whoever let themselves be lost for Christ's sake and for the gospel, they are safe.

It is a reversal of the fashion of this age when the mind insists, as St Paul insisted, that 'if boasting there must be, I will boast of the things that show up my weaknesses'.

It is a reversal of the fashion of this age when the mind knows, as St Francis of Assisi knew, that total poverty and simplicity are the greatest treasures in this world because they alone set us free to possess all things.

And finally, for Christian disciples who are supposed to know these truths, it is the greatest reversal of the fashion of this age when we see the one who has achieved the transfigured glory of a manhood made perfect in obedience to the Father, laying that glory aside just as the Eternal Word laid aside the glory of godhead, for us and for our salvation. A door had opened for him into heaven itself and he did not pass through it. The radiance faded from his face and the lines of weariness and pain returned.

His clothes were once more soiled and worn. And the greatest glory of all was his descent back to a lunatic boy and a lunatic world. That was the supreme transfiguration, reversing the fashion of this age through a mind re-made.

He calls us, as he called Peter, James and John, into that transfiguration through the re-making of our minds. 'If anyone wishes to follow me, let them leave self behind, take up their cross and come with me. If anyone wants to be first, let them make themselves last of all and servant of all.' We have to make a deliberate choice against the fashion of this age. Christ will take care of the re-making of our minds if we will only choose it.

And what a momentous choice it is. Today is the anniversary of what might be called the alternative transfiguration, when a radiance burned above Hiroshima three times brighter than the sun, and every material substance, every created thing was changed – that is the end towards which the fashion of this age, with all its ordinariness, its habitual assumptions, is driving God's world: not the re-making but the unmaking of his creation. On this anniversary we are confronted with the age-long choice between two fires: the fires of nuclear destruction or the fire of self-sacrifice and of ardent love and of renewal in the Holy Spirit.

'Don't take the fashion of this age as your pattern but be transfigured through the remaking of your minds.'

PART THREE

Passion and Crucifixion

Love's ultimate reality gazing at the Son
proclaims 'I AM'.
And He, as love's obedience,
responds, 'I will'.

13

The Man Who Was Born to Die

Eight Sundays ago it was Christmas Eve. Eight Sundays on from today it will be Easter Day. We are offering our worship and prayer in this service exactly halfway between the birth of Jesus and his death and resurrection. We look back to his coming into the world. We look forward to his dying for the world. And we are filled with thankfulness and adoration.

Now if I was talking about any other historical person you might say, So what? Every human life has a beginning and an end, but what's so special about that? It's true we learn the dates of important figures – Napoleon Buonaparte, 1769–1821; Queen Elizabeth I, 1558–1603. But those are the dates of her reign, of course. I don't remember when she was born. Because what matters is the things anyone does during a lifetime. The beginning and the end aren't all that significant. They're pretty much the same for all of us. We are all born, and we all die. It's what happens in between that distinguishes one from another.

But that isn't how Christians have talked about Jesus Christ; the very opposite, in fact. Have you ever noticed how strangely we run the words on in the Apostles' Creed: 'Born of the Virgin Mary; suffered under Pontius Pilate'. No mention of anything in between. And even more starkly, in the Nicene Creed we say: 'And was made man and was crucified', as though he were born to die. And it isn't only the brevity of the creeds, or some mistaken telescoping in later church doctrine, that accounts for this. We find the same bringing together of birth and death and resurrection in the New Testament. In the epistle to the Philippians we read: 'Being born in the likeness of men and being found in human form, he humbled himself in obedience to death, even death on a cross.' Again, in the first epistle of John we read that 'God loved us and sent his Son to be the expiation for our sins.' In fact, the earliest Christian writings, the epistles of Paul, expound the gospel with no reference whatever to the events of Jesus' life, as though all that matters is that he came into the world to redeem us through his death and his resurrection. Indeed, Paul specifically disowns any interest in the intervening years between that birth and that death. In 2 Corinthians 5.16 he says: 'Even though we have known, or understood, Christ after the flesh, yet now we know him in that way no more.'

Of course it was natural that new converts should want to know what manner of man their Risen Lord had been and what he had taught and done before his death. So the stories we have in the Gospels were passed on from the very beginning and later gathered together by the four evangelists. But even they were not writing a normal biography. St Mark's Gospel, which is reputed to reflect the way in which the apostle Peter told the stories to those who were being prepared for baptism, devotes almost one third of the book to the last five days of Jesus' life. And Luke, who deals extensively with the birth of Jesus, starts to tell of his last slow journey up to Jerusalem to die only seven chapters later, when there are still 15 to go. Can you think of any other life story in which such emphasis is given to the beginning, and especially to the end?

How can we today understand and explain why he came in order to die? There is so much that can be said and has been said. I want only to remind you of two of the many ways of looking at it.

First, our God is a forgiving God, a pardoning God. That is his nature from all eternity; but it is not an easy-going nature. Forgiveness is not the same as toleration; it is the opposite of overlooking any wrong. God in his mercy has made this world a moral order. There is a power built into it that restores the true balance if one species overreaches itself and demands too much. If we will insist on polluting our environment we shall destroy ourselves and the earth will be better without us. 'Whatsoever a man soweth, that shall he also reap.' The health of the whole depends on that. And if this is inexorable in the physical realm we can be sure it reflects the way things are in the spiritual realm. If God loves and forgives us he must do so in such a way that this moral order is not neutralized and the destructiveness of sin must be allowed to operate. Even in our human relationships true forgiveness does precisely that. Sin is allowed to bear its bitter fruit and work out its inherent destructiveness. But it is the one who forgives who, out of compassionate understanding of the wrongdoer, accepts the wound and the diminishment and the shock of that evil, and absorbs it in love and truth until the destructiveness of it is turned into new life. God's infinite and unchanging love takes something like that upon himself as the price foreseen of making a world in which sin is a necessary possibility. That is the Lamb slain, the sacrifice, in the heart of God, before the foundation of the world. But because the eternal truth of God must be manifested in time if it is to have any effect upon us creatures of time, 'God,' says St Paul, 'sending his own Son in a form like that of our own sinful nature and to deal with sin, has passed judgement against sin within that very nature so that the commandment of the law may work itself out fully in us.' 'For while we were yet sinners, Christ died for us, and that is God's own proof of his love for us.'

But there is another aspect of God's purpose in coming as the Word to be born and to die. It was not only for our forgiveness but also for our regeneration. 'Born that man no more may die', we sing at Christmas, 'Born to raise the sons of earth, Born to give them second birth.' And 'second birth' is what makes us the sons and daughters of God, with the image and likeness of God restored in us. 'He came to his own, but his own did not receive him; but to all those who did receive him he gave power to become children of God.' Now in order to understand that I invite you to look again at the significance of this halfway Sunday which draws the beginning and the end of Jesus' life together, and to recognize the horror with which thinking people recognize that each one of us, not only Jesus, is actually born to die. The Book of Ecclesiastes is there in the Bible to show that such a sense of futility in the face of death has overtaken people in all ages, but it is an obsession for many of today's writers. One of the characters in Samuel Beckett's play *Waiting for Godot* puts it brutally:

> Astride of a grave and a difficult birth. Down in the hole, lingeringly the grave-digger puts in the forceps. We have time to grow old. The air is full of our cries.

Another playwright, Tom Stoppard, wrote with the same sense of outrage about the way in which death treads upon the very heels of our birth. In his play, *Rosencrantz and Guildenstern Are Dead*, the courtier Rosencrantz says:

> We must be born with an intuition of mortality. Before we know the words for it, before we know that there are words, out we come, bloodied and squalling with the knowledge that for all the compasses in the world there's only one direction, and time is its only measure.

Forgive me for imposing these painful quotations on you. But we must let the cry of the world disturb our peace if we are to understand the gospel Jesus has brought to the world. For he knew how tortured men and women are by the waste and the futility of their few years of striving and clinging when death will so soon take all away, even the memory of what they have been. 'Whoever wants to preserve his life, his true self, will lose it; and whoever lets his life be lost for my sake and the gospel's, will save it. For what does it profit anyone to gain the whole world and forfeit his true self? And what can anyone give to buy back that lost self?'

Do you not see that this terrified inability to let one's self be lost, this desperate holding on to life, this anger at the brevity of existence, is the absolute opposite of God's total self-expenditure, his acceptance of the wound and diminishment of our sin, his giving away of himself in creation and redemption? Do you not see the contrast between our instinctive self-preservation and the mind of the eternal Son of God who did not count his divinity a thing to be grasped? When this Lord God created humanity in his own likeness, in his image, this is what he expected to see reflected there: the same readiness to let self go, to be given away out of love and thankfulness. But the Adam in you and me has been deceived into thinking that in order to be like God we must grasp more knowledge, more power, more self-importance. So we lost our likeness to our Father, and fell into anxiety, mistrust and obsessive self-preservation. Until God himself came among us as man to live out the divine self-abandonment in our frail flesh. 'A second Adam to the fight and to the rescue came.' In Jesus the image of our humble, self-giving God was perfectly restored in human nature. And to as many as received him and let their mind be made one with his mind, and his Spirit be made one with their spirit, to them he gave power to become, to be born as, God's children, bearing the same family likeness. 'The Son of Man,' that is, true humanity in him, and through him in us who believe, 'has not come to be served, to be treated as master, but to serve and to give up his life as a ransom for many.'

Perhaps you have wondered why I didn't contradict those examples of outrage over the fact that we seem to have been born to die by immediately referring to the resurrection: 'But we know that death is not the end. There is no futility in the shortness of our earthly lives since in Christ we have life everlasting.' Now of course that is true and I believe it. But unless we are very watchful over the thoughts of our hearts we may be using the sure and certain hope of resurrection as an escape from that dying, that losing of life which Jesus said is the way, the only way in which we can follow him. 'If any man would come after me, let him give up himself and take up his cross and follow me.' Not that we can die for the sins of the world; only the righteous one could do that. But there is plenty of dying to do if his mind is to become our own; there is a laying down of life before there can be any taking it up again. There is no short cut to resurrection.

Supposing a colleague at work had spread false rumours about you and so beaten you to an appointment you were expecting to get, and you said, 'Good luck to you, I hope you enjoy it. Promotion means nothing to me.' There would be no forgiveness in that, for instead of accepting and absorbing the wound you pretend it doesn't exist, and use your faith in resurrection as a kind of one-up-manship. Because you've got out of the dying, there's no new life. Suppose a friend loses her child in an accident, and you say, 'Trust in the Lord's wisdom. He has taken your little one to a far happier life than you could have given.' There is no comfort in that, no compassion, for you are not sharing her agony nor bearing her burden but trying to dismiss it. Because there's no dying for you in that, there's no resurrection in your words. Or suppose that your husband has retired from the life's work he loved, and you've even moved to another town. If you run around buying him new tools and a lawnmower, and pester him to join the local clubs, you mustn't be surprised if he seems in a daze. He needs to mourn, and to have you weep with him, for the death of so much that has been his very self. You too, perhaps, need to admit your deep bereavement of the home you made and have lost. Then, when you have done that bit of dying, you will find you have left it behind and a new life will begin naturally.

Through our common humanity we, like Jesus, are born to die and rise again, not once only at the end of this earthly life but again and again in a succession of lesser deaths that are nonetheless real deaths, whereby we learn the habit of giving ourselves up, letting them be lost, letting go, until we reflect, through Jesus Christ, the likeness of God, his Father and ours, who gives his very being away in love, eternally and inexhaustibly.

14

Sharing In and Sharing With

The Gospel according to St Luke is remarkable for the amount of material which the writer has derived from independent sources which were not, apparently, available to the other evangelists, though St John seems to have been acquainted with some of them. Among the passages peculiar to St Luke is that which describes a previous sharing of a cup of wine at the Last Supper before the more familiar narrative of the institution of the eucharist. This is how it is told in Luke 22.15–18:

> And he said to them: 'With desire I have desired to eat this Passover with you before my passion; for I tell you, never again shall I eat it until the time when it finds its fulfilment in the Kingdom of God.' And having received a cup and given thanks he said: 'Take this and share it out among yourselves; for I tell you, I shall drink no more from the fruit of the vine until the time when the Kingdom of God comes.'

This solemn and ritual reference to both eating and drinking lays the greatest possible emphasis upon a joyful anticipation of the coming Kingdom after an interval of passivity and pain. The note of expectation is also found in the Gospels of Mark and Matthew, but there it is tacked on at the end of the words of institution. Luke's version makes more of the fact that this was a Passover meal even though it may have been antedated, and therefore it followed the customary pattern of two cups of wine, ritually handed to the head of the family group, one early in the meal and the other towards the end. So it says quite correctly that he 'received' the cup. The Passover meal was a commemoration, but one which identified the participants with a people who were setting out upon a journey in an 'earnest looking forward' to the fulfilment of a great promise. So now, as an expression of his absolute confidence that the fulfilment is on the way, Jesus bids his friends share the cup between them, pledging themselves to the future.

65

It is a very significant word that Luke uses. It was already being used at that time in the Greek translation of the Old Testament to describe soldiers sharing out the spoil (Judges 5.30), or the carefully appointed largesse with which King David celebrated the arrival of the Ark of the Covenant when 'a flat loaf, a portion of meat and a cake of raisins' was given to each man and woman (2 Samuel 6.19). It speaks of anything that is shared out fairly from a common source, and is used in the Gospels to describe how the soldiers shared out the garments of the crucified Jesus.

There are two aspects in any such distribution. Several people are sharing *in* the one thing, be it a meal or a cup or a heap of clothes. And each one of them shares that one thing *with* all the others. Luke's word points to the sharing *with* – 'Take this and share it out among yourselves.' Paul, for whom the same thought is enormously important, emphasizes the sharing *in* – 'The cup of blessing which we bless, is it not a sharing, a communion, in the blood of Christ? The loaf which we break, is it not a sharing, a communion, in the body of Christ, seeing that one loaf, one body are we, the many? For we are all partakers from the one loaf.' So the many are made one by sharing *in* the one gift; but this can only happen when each one is willing to share the gift *with* the many others. And what enables us to share and so become one is the overriding urgency of our common hope. Because we are a people waiting with eager expectation and absolute confidence for a fulfilment, beyond the present moment, of all that has been promised and prayed for, we are inspired to share with one another everything God gives us during this waiting period.

For the word 'Take this and share it out among yourselves' obviously carried a very wide meaning for Luke. In the second chapter of Acts he uses the same word at two crucial points. In verse 3, in the account of the gift of the Holy Spirit, we read: 'And there appeared to them tongues like flames of fire, shared out among them and coming to rest upon each one.' It is an image of one fiery source from which each receives his or her portion. This accords very closely with Paul's teaching about the Spirit, which is closely parallel to his teaching about the one bread, one body. 'One body, one Spirit, even as also you were called in one hope of your calling' (Ephesians 4.4). 'All these gifts are the work of one and the same Spirit, distributing them separately to each individual at will' (1 Corinthians 12.11). It is as though Jesus Christ were saying to all of us concerning this supreme gift of the Holy Spirit which they have in common, 'Take this and share it out among yourselves.'

Later in the same chapter where Luke is describing the close-knit community of believers in Jerusalem, he says, 'All whose faith had drawn them together held everything in common and sold their possessions and goods and shared them out among all as the need of each required' (Acts 2.45). In this verse the two words we have already noticed are brought together. 'They held everything in common' means literally, 'They held everything in a sharing or communion', like the sharing *in* the body of Christ. And then what they shared *in* they also shared *with* one another. It was as though the Lord, receiving from them the common treasure of all that they had offered, said, 'Take this and share it out among your-selves.'

This principle of sharing in and sharing with is meant to be applied to every gift that we receive from God. No such gift is a private possession. The good news of salvation is something we share in, recognizing that others in their own way have shared in it as well and so, together with them all, endeavouring to share that gospel with all among whom we live.

The insights which come to us as we read the Bible or think about life or say our prayers are none of them a private illumination to be enjoyed on our own. They are a sharing in the wisdom and devotion which is God's continual gift to humanity in Christ, and each spark of under-standing which is given to us is meant to be shared with someone else. And in every such sharing each should be ready to receive something from the other.

Paul applies this principle of sharing in and sharing with to the gifts of ministry. Ministry, like the Holy Spirit, is the gift of the ascended Christ. 'Therefore it says, Having ascended into the heights he led captivity captive and gave gifts to men' (Ephesians 4.8). Then, in words reminiscent of the one fire dispersed upon the many waiting heads, he goes on: 'And he gave some apostles and some prophets and some evangelists and some pastors and teachers (yes, and he might have added, some martyrs also), to equip God's people for work in his service and for the building up of the body of Christ. 'The gift of ministry itself is no man or woman's pre-rogative. It is meant to be shared out among ourselves or it becomes an occasion for pride and turns rotten. There are no specialists in ministry.

But there are functionaries. We should not bemoan the fact that the church has become an institution, a framework for decision-making, discipline and the handing-on of the gospel tradition. Because our waiting for the fufilment is being prolonged through history these structures became necessary. But the authority and the decision-making is always to be regarded as functional. Someone among all those who share the gift of ministry is appointed to the role of leadership of one kind or another. This does not make him or her a better person, nor can it be regarded as a greater gift of ministry. It is a job which someone has to do. It may be shared or delegated, but may not be abdicated.

Ministry, however, is far wider than function and, like all the gifts of God, the sharing in it and the sharing of it with others takes place in the context of eager expectation. The waiting may be prolonged through history but the end is not in doubt. This great passage about the gift of ministry in the epistle to the Ephesians leads us back again to the undying hope – 'Until we all attain unto the oneness of faith and of the knowledge of God, unto mature manhood, unto the measure of the stature of the fulfilment of Christ.'

15

Behold Your God

'If I then, your Lord and Teacher, have washed your feet, you also ought
to wash one another's feet. For I have given you an example, that
you also should do as I have done to you.' (John 13.14,15)

An example to copy, yes, but far, far more than that. Jesus was not saying,
'See, I have set you a good example of humility – go and do likewise.' He
was saying, 'I have just shown you a faint reflection of God. Be perfect
with your heavenly Father's perfection.' What Jesus did for his disciples
in the Upper Room was to give them the ultimate truth about his
Father's love for them.

The manner in which the opening words of this chapter set the stage
makes this quite clear. First, we are led to expect the final revelation of
Christ's love for his own. He had always loved them and now he was to
show the uttermost extent of that love. But we are also carefully keyed
up for an ultimate unfolding of the secret of God himself. Jesus, we are
told, knew that God had entrusted to him the whole task of revelation.
He, like a true ambassador, had come from God and was soon to return
to God. There were only a few hours left and the moment had arrived
for the last veil to be drawn aside and the Creator's true nature disclosed.
So, without a word he rose from table, pulled off the seamless robe,
wrapped a towel round his waist, poured water into a basin and started
washing the disciples' feet. 'Behold your God.'

When the Son of God took the form of a household slave he lost
nothing of his godlikeness, for that is God's role. Every woman who turns
back to the kitchen when the guests have left to begin the washing up is
most like God at that moment. The cleaners who wake in the small hours
and walk the empty streets to clear up yesterday's mess in schools and
offices have more of God in their action than the head teacher or the
managing director. Like the patient seas in Keats' poem, 'the moving
waters at their priestlike task of pure ablution round earth's human
shores', our Creator has been cleaning up the mess, in ceaseless serving
love, from the beginning of time, for there is no-one else who can do it.
'If I do not wash you, you can have nothing in common with me.'

St John deliberately gives us this incident in place of the institution of the eucharist. He must have known about that event, for its constant repetition was already the central act of the young church's worship. He gives us this other event almost as though it were interchangeable with it. Indeed, the great commentator Bishop Westcott has deduced that the two events overlapped. He believed that the bread must already have been shared among them when Jesus rose from table and began washing their feet, and that the blessing and passing of the cup followed the departure of Judas Iscariot from the room. Be that as it may, the breaking and sharing of the bread and the pouring and giving of the wine make exactly the same disclosure of God our Father as the washing of the feet. God is he who gives himself in love. God is he who put himself out in service to his world. God is he who is wounded for our healing, broken for our forgiving. God is he who shares himself in an eternal exchange of life for life, a ceaseless interflow of love and belonging.

When you feel resentful, as we all do, over the chores of your inescapable service of other people, look again at the broken bread and outpoured wine. And when, having given that service, you are hurt or angry because it was not acknowledged or was taken for granted, look upon the basin and the towel.

Philip said to him, 'Lord, show us the Father and we ask no more.' Jesus answered, 'Have I been all this time with you, Philip, and you still do not know me? Anyone who has seen me has seen the Father.'

16

From the Same Cup

A good private secretary is a treasure beyond price. But from time to time she or he is called on to meet outrageous demands with infinite patience. At such moments the secretary's only meagre consolation lies in feeling somewhat privileged, more in the know and closer to events than anyone else.

Such a one was Baruch, secretary and personal assistant to the prophet Jeremiah. He was as sorely tried as any secretary could be. On one occasion Jeremiah dictated all the major pronouncements he had made in the past year or more till they filled a single great scroll. It was political dynamite, exposing the sickness of society, and its impending collapse. Jeremiah reckoned the popular mood was such that his words might be listened to this time, especially if he did not provoke police action by appearing in public himself. So poor Baruch was sent to read his scroll in the open piazza between the temple and the palace. The risk paid off, because he was able to disclaim authorship. He was made to read it again before the privy council, on whom it made a deep impression.

But when this was reported to the king and Baruch had to repeat it all for a third time, after every fresh three or four columns had been read, the king leaned forward, coolly sliced off the length of unrolled parchment and tossed it onto the fire. By the time the great indictment had been completed the whole painstaking manuscript had gone up in flames. And then, no sooner were Jeremiah and Baruch smuggled away into safe hiding than the prophet dictated the whole thing all over again to his exhausted secretary. No wonder Baruch comforted himself with the certainty that such faithfulness would be rewarded.

But Jeremiah's great heart is breaking at the thought of his people's doom. He is totally involved in their folly and its inevitable outcome, and Baruch's self-pity and private ambition seem at that moment cruelly inappropriate. 'Thus says the Lord, the God of Israel, to you Baruch. You

have said, "Woe is me. I am weary with my groaning and I find no rest."
Behold – what I have built I am breaking down, and what I have planted
I am plucking up – that is, the whole land. And do you seek great things
for yourself? Seek them not. For, behold, I am bringing evil upon all
flesh, says the Lord. But I will give you your life, as a prize of war, in all
places to which you may go.'

That little chapter of only five verses – Jeremiah 45 – was full of meaning for Dietrich Bonhoeffer. In the letters he wrote from prison he
referred to it more often than any other Bible text. 'We feel,' he wrote
about it, 'how closely our own lives are bound up with other people's.'
On the day after his own death became certain, 21 July 1944, he wrote:
'It is only by living completely in this world that one learns to have faith.
One must completely abandon any attempt to make something of oneself, whether it be a saint, or a converted sinner, or a churchman …
taking seriously, not our own sufferings, but those of God in the world –
watching with Christ in Gethsemane … that is how one becomes human
and a Christian' (cf. Jer. 45).'

It is typical of the spiritual discernment of church liturgy at its best that
that little chapter is set as one of the readings for the commemoration of
the apostle James. It exactly foreshadows that story in the Gospels in
which James and his brother John sought great things for themselves,
or were perhaps embarrassed by their mother doing so on their behalf.
This also was an occasion of impending judgement for Jerusalem, for
humankind, and the prophet who had warned them was on his way to
take upon himself the doom of the city, the sins of the world. And with
unbelievable insensitivity the sons of Zebedee chose this moment to ask
for their reward – the two places of highest honour in his Kingdom.

Amazingly, Jesus took them seriously. Their hope, like Baruch's, was
hope for the wrong thing, but there was faith in it, and love for him. So
he took them seriously in order to take them further. 'Are you able to
drink the cup that I drink, not calling down fire upon those who reject
us, but taking into yourselves the wrongs of the world and the awful
outcome of them? Are you able to be baptized with the baptism I am
baptized in, immersed in humanity and its catastrophe so as to lift it with
me into rebirth?' They answered, 'We are able', and, though they didn't
understand what they were saying, he believed them. For that had always
been his hope. That is why he had chosen the Twelve in the first place.

I don't know when he first realized for certain that they were not
going to go through it with him, and that strangers were to be on his
right hand and his left as he entered, through agony, into his Kingdom.

But even when he knew he had to go forward alone, his faith in them was not withdrawn. The cup that I drink you will drink, if not now, then some day when you are ready. And the baptism, the immersion into death which is mine, will be yours too after my resurrection has given you my strength and my Spirit. Paul takes up this daring theme also: 'For if we have been united with him in a resurrection like his' – great things, not for ourselves, but for 'the whole land'. With even greater daring the epistle to the Colossians has the words: 'This is my way of helping to complete, in my poor human flesh, the full tale of Christ's afflictions still to be endured, for the sake of his body which is the church.'

This is a facet of the glory of the church which we have ignored. We are called to share and bear the cross as an inescapable part of our involvement in the destiny of man and as a necessary condition of the world's salvation. The sign of the cross given at baptism can mean no less than this. The sharing of the cup at communion pledges us to sacrifice for the redemption of all things. The fellowship of his sufferings and the power of his resurrection are inseparable and he wants us to be with him in both.

17

Christ Handed Over

Of all the various presents that may be given to any of us, at Christmas or at any other time, the ones that mean most are those which have actually belonged to the person who gives them. It may be an heirloom from a godmother's jewellery box or a favourite Dinky car from a small boy's collection: the fact of its having been owned and loved by the giver adds a value that money cannot buy. There is a difference between giving and handing over.

It was just such a handing over as this that took place in the incarnation. 'He that spared not his own Son but delivered him up, or handed him over, for us all, how shall he not also with him freely give us all things, how can he fail to lavish upon us all he has to give?' In the birth of Jesus that which was most precious to God, his only-begotten Son, his very self, changed hands and was given up.

The handing over of the Son of God is a central theme of the Gospels and a turning point in the story. 'The Son of Man,' says Jesus in Mark, 'shall be handed over, delivered up, to the chief priests and scribes and they shall condemn him and shall hand him over to the Gentiles.' And later in the same gospel Mark tells how they bound Jesus and handed him over to Pilate, and Pilate, when he had scourged him, handed him over to be crucified. Tied up like a parcel and passed from hand to cruel hand – that is what it meant to be handed over. The men who wrote the Gospels used this phrase 'handed over' so often in their story of the passion of Jesus that it clearly had a strong theological significance for them. It means something far wider and more mysterious than the betrayal by Judas Iscariot; that was only the beginning of a complete transposition of Jesus out of his own freedom and initiative and intense activity, and into the grasp and compulsion and will of others. 'God spared not his own Son but handed him over for us all.'

I am speaking of the passion – the passivity – of Christ at the Christmas season. Why? Because the very beginning of any human life has this in common with the very end – you are carried. Things are done to you. The infant and the geriatric are literally in other people's hands. So Christmas night may also be described as 'the same night in which he was handed over'. This is the paradox of the incarnation: that the Maker of all things is constricted in a crib, the Eternal Word has not yet learned to talk, and he who holds us in existence must be carried and kept safe. Here too we see the transfer of the Son of God from pure freedom to constraint, from creative energy to passivity, from initiative to waiting. 'God spared not his own Son but handed him over for us all.'

But what does it mean, this talk about God's own Son? We distort the true faith and miss the point if we allow ourselves to imagine anything like three Gods. Whatever we say about the Son of God we are saying it about God. The Son of God is God being obedient to his own nature. The Son of God is God under the constraints he has set for himself. The Son of God is God eternally tying his own hands with love and handing himself over for us all. The handing over of the Son of God was not a brief unique incident lasting from about 5 BC to AD 30. It is an eternal truth about God, but we should never have guessed it if we had not seen his overwhelming glory in the helplessness of Bethlehem and the help-lessness of the judgement hall and the cross.

The living God passes our understanding and stretches like a horizon beyond our newest, clearest thought of him. But this we know: he is like an artist and he is like a lover, and both are bound and handed over. The artist, in choosing to express himself in something that is not himself, but stone or sound or colour, has committed himself to an activity which cannot be the smooth unfolding of a premeditated plan but must inevitably involve coming to terms with the materials he has chosen, getting things right as he goes along, and an inexhaustible patience and resourcefulness, struggle and cost. The lover, unless his love is false, has by the act of loving given to some other being the power to disappoint him infinitely. Both the lover and the artist have tied their own hands. They have passed over from power to depend-ence, from doing to being done to, from achievement to waiting. And pre-cisely by letting that happen to them their true nature, their glory, is revealed. As artist or as lover they have handed themselves over, made a present of them-selves and let the most essential, precious thing that is theirs change hands.

That is what God has been doing from before the foundation of the world. 'He that spared not his own Son, his own self, but handed himself over for us all, how can he fail to lavish upon us all he has to give?'

No, he cannot help but give and give again, and wait and wait for our response. And what is that response to be when we have at last understood?

Not a busy programme of service and achievement. Why should our agenda be so different from his? He who is waiting for the world's response asks above all else that we share the waiting. 'Could you not watch with me one hour?' He who entered into his glory when he passed from splendid doing into shameful being-done-to calls us to stand by him in his silence and inaction. If we do so we shall find ourselves in a large company today. And our prayer will grow more like the spontaneous movements of those who watch a sculptor at work and tense their own muscles in sympathy with his concentration, or like those who hold their breath to see whether the mail includes the letter their friend has been waiting for. 'Thy Kingdom come, thy will be done,' is that kind of prayer. So, in the time before Christmas, the best present we can prepare to hand over to him, the one that most evidently belongs to us and is typical of us, is the unfulfilled longing that we share with him. Let us stay, then, in the posture of Advent, waiting upon the eternally patient God with the love that bears all things, believes all things, hopes all things, endures all things.

18

Christ the King

In the days of Jesus a monarch was expected to be not the representative of a nation but its god. From Julius Caesar onwards temples were built for the worship of the emperor as soon as he had died and in some cases while he was still alive. Emperors held their empire by force of arms, and lesser local kings like Herod and Agrippa were watched suspiciously, and kept their thrones only by paying great sums to the emperor's treasury. So Annas and Caiaphas knew that to accuse Jesus of claiming to be a king was enough to make the Governor, Pilate, distrust him from the start. Jesus tries to get Pilate to realize that that may be what they were up to. 'Are you the King of the Jews?' 'Do you ask this of your own accord or have others talked about me?' 'Am I a Jew? Your people, your high priests, have handed you over to me.' 'Mine is not a Kingdom of this world. If it were, my followers would have fought to prevent my arrest. But my Kingdom isn't of this kind, your kind.'

Shouldn't that have satisfied Pilate? It might have done so if Jesus meant what the church has often thought he meant by 'not of this world'. Politicians love it when the church talks about heaven. It makes them feel safe from interference. As long as Jesus rules from heaven over a Kingdom not of this world, they can get on with ruling the things that *are* of this world.

But Jesus didn't mean that at all. When Jesus spoke about something that is not of this world, he was thinking of that part of every human being which lies beyond the immediate demands and instincts and interests of the body and mind. Call it the soul or spirit of humanity so long as you include in it the vivid experiences of beauty, the urge to create and discover and the capacity for idealism, self-sacrifice and awe. These are the timeless elements in human nature, the factors that can't be summoned up at will or produced by anyone else. They are the material to which Christ appeals and from which he builds his Kingdom of humble revolutionaries here and now.

Pilate at least was sharp enough to see that Jesus wasn't talking about heaven. He was talking about a real band of followers. 'So you are a king, then?' he asks. And Jesus cannot deny it, though he realizes that this Roman will never grasp what he means. So he answers: 'King is your word, but yes, I am a king of sorts. That is why I was born into this world, to bear witness to the truth and *all* who are on the side of truth listen to my voice,' answer my call, become my Kingdom.

Years ago I heard of a woman visiting her 14-year-old son during his first term in a boarding school, and being very disturbed at finding the walls of his study adorned with pictures from a 'girlie' magazine. She confided her anxiety to one of his godfathers, who said: 'You've no need to worry; he didn't bother to take them down before you arrived.' When Christmas came, the boy received from his godfather a very fine framed print of the head of a girl by Rembrandt, and proudly took it back to school at the end of the holidays. Six months later, when his mother went to the school prize-giving in the summer term, Rembrandt had the walls to himself. 'I was born into the world to bear witness to the truth. All who are on the side of the truth listen to my voice.'

I feel there must have been a long pause before that troubled Governor murmured the question that plagues every judge both then and now: 'What is truth?' For he had listened to the voice that was calling him and he gave the right verdict: 'No case to answer.' But then he listened to the voice of the rulers of this world – and so do we. So, unfortunately, does the church, again and again.

19

God's Catalyst

'Now is the judgement of this world, now shall the ruler of this world be cast out, and I, when I am lifted up from the earth, will draw all to myself.'
(John 12.31–32)

Among human beings there are some men and women, and there always have been all through history, who have the gift of courageous honesty, an embracing love and a great simplicity. They may be as different as Francis of Assisi and Joan of Arc, Mahatma Gandhi, Dom Helder Camara or Archbishop Desmond Tutu. You may know someone who has those gifts of uncompromising truth, embracing love and total simplicity, who is not at all famous, for most of them remain hidden. You may even know a child or a teenager who has this effect. Whoever they are, and however they differ from one another, they have the same tragic effect upon the rest of us. They long to draw us all together and unite us in their vision of the truth, yet in fact they divide us more sharply into opposing factions. They don't set out to drive us into opposite camps. But by setting the truth before us, by demonstrating the demands of love, by simply being what they are, they compel the rest of us to choose either to follow their truth or to reject it. Such people are God's catalysts. They bring things to a head. They force a decision.

This quality in all such people is a pale reflection of what we meet in Jesus Christ. He supremely and purely was God's truth in every thought of his and every action; he was God's embracing love in every relationship he made with people; he was God's unarmed simplicity in the midst of this confused and devious world. And just by being these things he forced his contemporaries to show their true colours. Just by being himself in our midst he still forces us all to choose either to respond or to reject what he stands for. We declare our choice concerning Jesus not by the opinions we hold about him but by the obedience we offer him. There are those who argue that in a multi-cultural society embracing various faith traditions it is no longer appropriate to test people with the question, 'What do you think of Christ?' Jesus agreed with that. 'Not everyone who says to me Lord, Lord, shall enter God's Kingdom, but he who does my Father's will.'

What was at stake in the judgement hall on the first Good Friday morning was not what Caiaphas and Pilate and the motley crowd said about Jesus when confronted by his truth, but what they did in response to that truth. That is how we accept or reject him still. He sees the man in our street who is odd man out for some reason – his race maybe. He sees the relative with whom we have had a long-standing rift. 'I must reach out and include them among my friends,' says Jesus. Do we follow him? He learns of some injustice inflicted on a family too weak to defend itself. 'I must expose and withstand this wrong,' says Jesus. Do we stand with him then? 'Don't mix politics with religion,' cry the powers-that-be. Jesus retorts, 'This is not politics but people, and my Father's love for them.' The church authorities suggest judiciously that these issues are more complex than we might suppose, and while there is no common mind, Christians should not act unilaterally so as to endanger the unity of the fellowship. Jesus answers, 'Do not think that I have come to bring peace, but a sword. I have come to set a man against his father, and a daughter against her mother, and a daughter-in-law against her mother-in-law, and a man's foes will be those of his own household.'

It is not that Jesus Christ took any pleasure in setting his contemporaries at odds. Peace was his gift and he longed to guide their feet into the way of peace. But peace is the fruit of justice. Peace is the child of truth and love. And when he sets God's truth and God's love in our midst most of us find it too threatening. 'This is the judgement, that the light has come into the world, and men loved darkness rather than light, because their deeds were evil.'

The easy-going world prefers not to talk in such stark contrasts of light and dark, good and evil, God and the devil. It is more civilized to tone down the colours, blur the definitions and live with half truths. Then no one need be condemned and no one need be saved. That is the spirit of the world, and its toleration is very attractive.

But Jesus' love, God's love in him, could not stand that sort of tolerance. He knew that men and women were the children of God. He was here to give them power to become what they were made to be. He must offer them salvation though it opened the possibility of damnation. He must draw them into his bliss, though it might drive them into despair. The same force of electro-magnetism that draws some particles irresistibly towards it, repels others. The combination of divine truth, love and simplicity in Jesus which gripped John and James and held Peter through his failure and Thomas through his doubt, was too much for Judas and drove him into the dark, so far, at least, as we are told. And Jesus knew that this is the way it must be. 'I did not come to judge the world but to save the world. He who rejects me, and does not receive my sayings, has a judge. The word that I have spoken will be his judge on the last day.'

Year after year Good Friday confronts us with the choice that confronted Pilate and Caiaphas, yes, and the fickle crowd, in the hall of judgement. 'Whom do you want me to release unto you: this man or Barabbas?' The choice is our judgement, our ordeal, again and again. But for Jesus it did not remain an eternally open question. He had more confidence of the ultimate outcome than we dare claim for ourselves. He will never compel our choice. Love and truth and simplicity must leave us free, must put him at risk. Yet he goes his way knowing that the outcome is sure. 'I, when I am lifted up from the earth, will draw all to myself.'

20

The Seven Last Words

In the form for which Haydn was originally commissioned to compose his work, it was intended that, after the introductory movement, each of the remaining seven should be preceded by a brief address, so that both words and music should concentrate upon each of the traditional 'words' from the cross in turn. Haydn's music naturally reflects the dramatic and devotional approach to the story of Christ's crucifixion which was characteristic of the baroque period. A modern style of meditation that interposed more of our contemporary questions would have struck a false note. By listening again and again to the music, I have tried to allow Haydn himself to suggest these thoughts and images to me.

1. 'Father, forgive them, for they know not what they do.'
   Pater, dimitte illis, quia nesciunt quid faciunt

Nothing but questions: however you look at it, that is the effect of the story of Christ's crucifixion. It raises to an acute degree all the questions about unmerited suffering, injustice and responsibility which are stirred up whenever we confront the strength of evil. The questions rise and waver and fall back unanswered, and the only unambiguous sound is the voice of inhumanity and the lie.

The crucifixion of Jesus Christ was not more outrageous than all other crimes against justice, truth or innocence: it simply summed them up. And because of the character of this victim and what he made of his death, he is the representative for all time of the conflict between hatred and love, between ultimate evil and goodness. As so often, the conflict seems very uneven. Goodness, gentleness and faith stand unarmed and at risk amid the opposing forces. If there is any answer in this event it does not lie on the surface; it comes out of the darkness of seeming defeat.

There is something else that comes out of the darkness when evil overreaches itself: Nemesis. That idea is hateful to us, yet strangely reassuring. Nemesis insists there is a limit to the spread of evil, because evil ultimately brings about its own destruction. Just as individual victims of injustice feel within themselves a sense of outrage swelling to breaking point, so, on a cosmic scale, the rhythm of history brings an eventual turning of the tide, as retribution and purgation sweep back over the corrupted land.

But the heavy, irrevocable tread of justice marching back is matched by a miraculous cry rising from the cross of Jesus Christ, no less insistent: *Dimitte illis! Dimitte illis!* Forgive them, these very ones, whoever they may be, who at this moment in time are blindly collaborating in the universal wrong. Forgive *them*. The faint, unceasing voice of understanding love contends against the voice of judgement: God in humanity pleading with God in destiny. Forgiveness doesn't make light of evil. It knows the swelling sense of outrage, the shock and shame of injury. But, instead of throwing it back or nursing the grievance, forgiveness transforms it and turns the event of utmost evil into the occasion of utmost good.

2. 'Today thou shalt be with me in paradise.'
   Hodie mecum eris in Paradiso

Any acute ordeal, as it drags on, cuts you off, because no-one else can know what you are going through or share it with you. A man dying in pain and in public represents extreme loneliness, being surrounded by people who are watching, but totally detached from his torment and his slow descent into death. For someone to break out of that isolation so as to make a perfect communication with another person in the same affliction is a marvel of selfless compassion.

It is quite extraordinary that the silence of Jesus should have conveyed such a current of sympathy to the criminal hung on another cross at his side as to evoke from him that basic cry for recognition: 'Remember me.' Whatever the man meant by that, he was answered with complete understanding and emphatic reassurance. But what could Jesus offer him that made any difference now? The promise of Paradise? What would that do for an embittered crook? 'Today with me' – '*Hodie mecum*': that is what every human being in the final resort most needs to hear: that he is not, after all, totally alone. 'Today with me' – with me in this pain, as though the whole world held nothing but our two crosses; with me beyond the pain, because we who have so strangely met, and at such depth, can never again be separate. '*Hodie mecum*.'

That assurance of another's care is all the paradise the man needs. '*Hodie mecum*' – the words echo in his mind like a song, and seem for a moment to bring him within sight and sound of the green coolness and the streams of the Garden. Others *in extremis* have experienced the same comfort. Call it escapism if you must; it continues to take people by surprise when they are in greatest need. The victim of a painful illness has written: 'There are times when I seem to be lifted above it all, and that lifting is like an invitation to the dance.'

As the horror of affliction sweeps back, of course, it is hard to cling to any faith. But whatever level of disbelief is plumbed, at each new depth of need the presence of that Other is reaffirmed. 'Today with me, even in the impossibility of believing it.'

3. 'Woman, behold thy son. Behold thy mother.'
   Mulier, ecce filius tuus

In our day the most widely-known religious picture is the Christmas card: Mary, Joseph and the baby. The centre piece for medieval society was a different trio, the three figures on the rood screen of every church: the crucified Jesus, the mother and the disciple. Both of them gaze at him alone: he completes the triangle by turning them to face one another. That is the true Holy Family.

For all that the natural family of parents and children gives us, it is a mixed blessing. It is the place where we learn to love and to distrust love, where we are both cherished and crippled. This comes about because we build our homes upon possessiveness and dependence. One might almost say that Jesus and his mother invented a new kind of family.

The Gospels tell us very little about their relationship, but the shared memories of 30 years must have made a powerful bond. We are left with an impression of a highly charged detachment between them which found expression in the word 'Woman' by which Jesus addressed his mother, courteously remote, yet resonant with associations – 'Woman', the name by which Adam first greeted the partner who was so much a part of himself; 'Woman', a word that embraces all her roles, as mother, sister, wife, child, lover.

As a celibate is free to love ardently all men and women, so this mother and Son, surrendering possessiveness, could adopt humankind as their family. The cost of that repeated surrender is indicated in this deliberate farewell.

I still cannot hear the words, 'Behold your Son', without supposing that he is speaking of himself: 'Look at me now.' It comes as a jolt to recall that he is thinking only of them, and the emphatic 'Your *son*' – which Haydn underlines in the long drawn five-note '*f-i-l-i-u-s*' – is the disciple at her side to whom he is now directing her. 'Woman, look, your son.' Woman to him, but mother to John and to every other disciple for all time. 'Behold, your mother.'

So he gave them to each other and wove their lives together like a duet. As he watched them go, Jesus saw his church being born, God's many sons and daughters brought into the glory of that same surrendering love, spreading, blossoming across the world, the fruit of his sacrifice and hers.

> 4. 'My God, my God, why hast thou forsaken me?'
>   *Deus meus, Deus meus, utquid dereliquisti me?*

St Mark's Gospel says that after the first three hours it became dark for three more. So far he has been simply enduring, though with a superbly selfless awareness of others. Now he is dying, and for anyone that means a withdrawal into aloneness, alone with whatever Presence there may be in the darkness. He of all men could go forward unafraid, for he had lived in an unbroken communion with the God he called Father. He had not expected to be saved from this death, but he had trusted that God would be with him to the end. Now there was no presence, no answer, no meaning to it all. The vast emptiness echoed back his cry with a more savage mockery than the earlier laughter of his tormentors. This was the worst betrayal of all.

The childlike faith of Jesus reached out into that dreadful void, fragile filaments of trust groping, and finding nothing there. Why, for what purpose, hast thou forsaken me, left me derelict? *Dereliquisti me?* The precious words from the cross reveal the almost unearthly perfection of a figure of the past; this raw cry of despair makes him one with our century. The question, 'Why? For what conceivable reason?' is the one which, more than any other, takes God away, makes him impossible. That is the point at which suffering becomes affliction. The afflicted, by being God-forsaken, lose all sight of their own value and significance. If they cannot harden and shrivel their hearts, they take upon themselves the universal worthlessness of existence. They carry the sin of the world.

Traditional Christianity has said that that is what this man did, not in fantasy but reality. How you identify his descent into dereliction with God's love for humanity is for you to decide. What is incontestable is that many who, in the extremity of suffering or despair, found no other comfort, have been able to say, 'That one has been there too', and however they explain his death, have discovered through it a God who still is credible.

5. 'I thirst.'
   Sitio

The cry for drink is the elemental cry of the infant for the mother. Jesus
has called for the divine Father and found himself abandoned. Now he
reverts to the instinctive craving for the human mother, and she has gone.
He is in utter need.

He had said once that no one who gave even a cupful of cold water
to some unimportant person, one of his 'little people', as he called them,
would go unrewarded. It sounded simple enough. Yet tens of thousands
of those little people have died this year for want of water. Of course their
need calls for a vast amount of money and organization. But these are
always forthcoming for the things that matter to the people in power.
The one thing that can break the deadlock is as simple and as precious as
clear water. Its name is 'caring'.

Thirst was one of the cruellest features of crucifixion, swinging the
clouded mind between tormenting mirages of water dripping into clear
pools or rising to the brim as a vessel is filled, and frantic, raging desire.
There was a jug of sour, watered wine among the soldiers' kit. There was
also a little spring of human caring not completely dried up. One of the
guards stood up, stooped and stretched up to serve the dying man.

That exchange of care from person to person, wherever it happens, is
the Kingdom of his Father for which he lived and died. The significance
of his life and death is summed up in the word 'thirst'. His consuming
desire for God, his passion for the Kingdom, on earth as in heaven, his
longing to make the little people his friends and win their response –
these are his thirst, and these his satisfaction and his rest.

6. 'It is finished.'
   Consummatum est

There is a breathtaking splendour in St John's account of the end. Like a
long-distance runner, Jesus gathers such life as remains in him and
expends it all in the finish. He takes death into his own hands and makes
of it a deliberate act. Every nerve of the tortured body knows that the
ordeal is over. He shouts his victory, and sinks into almost languorous
release. Hours before, he had invited the crucified thief to dance with
him into Paradise, and now that dance begins.

What he lays down is not just the heavy load of conflict and pain, but
a task completed and a mission accomplished in the creation of a new
relationship between humanity and God. He had said, 'It is my meat and

drink to do the will of him who sent me until I have finished his work.'
Now the exhausted wrestler senses there is no opposing resistance left;
the battle with evil is won for ever.

'*Consummatum est*.' Henceforth that word is the ground bass to all
existence and we live in a redeemed universe.

That rounded completeness after so short and circumscribed a life puts
to shame our wasted time. Whenever the end will come for us, we know
that what we have to offer up will be unfinished business, loose ends,
unkept promises. Our shame will mostly lie not in the evil we have done
but in the things we have left undone. To face death is to know non-
fulfilment as the very law of our existence. Yet this is not the last word
about any of us. To each individual life-story of incompleteness, and to
the whole history of this broken world, he has added his own full and
complete humanity; and since his spirit is at large in our midst, our story
is his story. Even now we experience those fleeting moments of illumination, when it seems that the universe takes up his loud cry that all shall
be well, and we know that, despite all tragedy and disappointment, the
last word will be *his* word: *Consummatum est*.

7. 'Father, into thy hands I commend my spirit.'
   In manus tuas, Domine, commendo spiritum meum

According to St Luke's account the words of Christ from the cross began
and ended with the word 'Father': 'Abba'. It was the name that summed
up his relationship with God. Even when he repeats the familiar night
psalm, 'Into thy hands, O Lord', he substitutes the word 'Father' – which,
incidentally, Haydn has observed, for he too keeps the familiar liturgical
rhythm of 'in manus tuas, Domine' by placing the poignancy of two notes
upon the first syllable of the word 'pater'. Pater, Abba, the almost childish
name by which it seems he had invariably addressed God, until that anni-
hilating onset of darkness three hours earlier, when he cried to the empty
silence, 'God, God, why?'

Nothing had changed since that forsakenness, nothing but a brief
easing of the parched throat. Yet now, with stupendous trust, he casts
himself into hands that are not there, like a child jumping from a window
in the dark: 'Look out there, I'm coming. Catch me!' It is as though his
insistent faith had recreated God – 'Into your hands, Father, I commend
my spirit.'

At the beginning it was the rest of us he was thinking about – 'Father,
forgive them.' That prayer had been answered forever, and now his
thought is fixed on the Father alone and his own home-coming. 'Your

hands, my spirit.' The faint pulse falters, the flame sinks; but his spirit is already soaring towards that reunion like a lark ascending. So Jesus dies into God.

Yet they *had* murdered him. Jew and Roman murdered the truth that had challenged them, and so do we. When conscience is killed the fabric of the world does begin to fall apart. The earthquake which is said to have followed the death of Jesus is symbolic, and what it symbolizes is the unmaking of the creation. Dead and living mingle in senseless confusion because there are no longer any distinctions between life and death, or between light and darkness, or between good and evil.

Then was his prayer for the forgiveness of the world one which, by the tragic nature of things, could not be granted? Is Nemesis after all irreversible? Yes, it is. For the rejection of God and the crucifixion of truth and love must lead back to chaos and nothingness. But remember, it was out of chaos, out of nothingness, that the universe was created at the first. And now, out of the dark dissolution of Christ's death, the hands of the Creator were about to start fashioning a New Man and a new beginning. The earthquake is the herald of the resurrection.

21

Pietà

Like so many of Michelangelo's greatest sculptures, his third *Pietà*, the dead Christ in the arms of his mother Mary, is in a very incomplete state, yet it says more than most of the world's great works of religious art. As a man of the Renaissance Michelangelo had deliberately turned away from the lean spiritualized figures of Gothic art and sought to express the ultimate inner truths through the physical weight and muscular tension of the human body. His two earlier works convey the massive, downward drag of the dead limbs. It is clear that in this last one also – the *Rondanini Pietà*, now in Milan – Michelangelo intended to create the same inert weight that the virgin can hardly manage to support. But he has changed his mind and pared down the body of our Lord, all but one great dangling arm, leaving a thin, curved figure of Gothic slenderness which, while retaining all the pathos of dissolution, seems already to be caught in an upward motion, as though death were turning into resurrection before our very eyes.

This is the mystery which the church, like Mary, carries before the eyes of humankind, the secret that Christians have been given to share with the world. Dying and rising are two sides of one unbroken motion like the fall and lift of a swooping gull. Yet the death is a total loss and extinction, no less real than the life into which it leads. This is the natural pattern of existence itself, the only way into fulfilment, though we persistently deny it, and this is the pattern which God in Christ endured and disclosed once and for all. His cross and resurrection is the very heart of all truth. It is the message we must never tire of sharing with humankind.

If we follow the way of cross and resurrection, we shall have to face a series of 'little deaths', each accompanied by real loss and tears and fear of the future. It happens when one's child first leaves home to go to school; when one breaks off a seemingly enriching relationship for the sake of fidelity; when circumstances change one's direction from a promising career into a more humdrum path. These are the memorable signposts, but along the whole length of the road there are numberless tiny deaths in which, through loss or disappointment, something of oneself perishes. In every such experience the deprivation can be foreseen in painful detail, while the promise of greater fulfilment afterwards is vague and unconvincing. So it was for Jesus. He could accurately anticipate his betrayal to the religious leaders, the sentence of death, his handing-over to the Romans, the flogging, humiliation and execution; but of what lay beyond he could give no detail but the bare statement of faith that after three days he would rise again (Mark 10.33, 34).

Saying 'No' to something we long to have is dreadfully difficult because we can see it so vividly and feel so keenly the pain of letting it go. Human beings are made to say 'Yes' rather than 'No'. Just as the dying is real but needs to be seen as the way into resurrection, so the 'No' is real, excruciatingly real, but needs to be drowned in the sound of the greater 'Yes'. This is how Jesus faced his temptations. When he put aside the turning of stones into bread, even to feed other hungry people, he was saying a resounding 'Yes' to the wholeness of man who must never be reduced to servility. When Jesus said 'No' to a dazzling display of power he was saying 'Yes' to man's freedom to think and respond for himself. And when he rejected the devil's methods of winning the kingdoms of the world he was saying 'Yes' to God's way of winning the world, which involves the cross and resurrection.

So the negative is always subservient to the positive. We let something slip from our hands in order to be free to grasp a new and greater gift. We die in order to live more fully, over and over again. And if during the years that are given to us we can form an instinctive habit of death and resurrection, then when the final, unavoidable letting-go is demanded of us we shall be able to accept it quite naturally with sure and certain hope: 'Welcome, life!'

PART FOUR

Resurrection and Ascension

Lord Jesus Christ,
alive and at large in the world,
help me to follow and find you there today,
in the places where I work,
meet people,
spend money,
and make plans.

Take me as a disciple of your Kingdom,
to see through your eyes,
and hear the questions you are asking,
to welcome all others with your trust and truth,
and to change the things that contradict God's love,
by the power of the cross
and the freedom of your Spirit.

22

Christt at Both Ends of the Line

'They [that is, two or three women] went into the tomb, where they saw a youth sitting on the right-hand side, wearing a white robe; and they were dumbfounded. But he said to them, "Fear nothing; you are looking for Jesus of Nazareth, who was crucified. He has been raised again; he is not here; look, there's the place where they laid him. But go and give this message to his disciples and Peter: 'He is going on before you into Galilee; there you will see him, as he told you.'" Then they went out and ran away from the tomb, beside themselves with terror.' (Mark 16.5–8)

Well, wouldn't you be terrified to find a grave you were visiting in a cemetery opened and empty, and a rather unaccountable and blunt young man passing on a message like that? No wonder they said nothing to anybody at first. Not only was the message unbelievable. The casual way in which it was delivered was almost equally unbelievable – 'Gone away. Meet you in Galilee.'

So death couldn't hold him, hatred and injustice couldn't destroy him. He was alive and at large in the world. One might meet him anywhere, just when he was most needed. Then why Galilee in particular? Galilee was at the other end of the map, a bit further from Jerusalem than Winchester is from London.

We know, of course, from the other familiar stories of the resurrection that he appeared to them before ever they started to obey that message. But this was a modification of his original Easter plan, a concession to their weakness. Because they would not take the road to the north and hurry back to the cornfields and fishing grounds of Galilee to find him there, he searched them out in that upper room where they had locked themselves in for fear, in the city that reeked of death. But his first plan still stood. 'He is going on before you into Galilee; there you will see him, as he told you.'

That summons and that promise are of immense significance for all who would like to be his disciples today, for the credibility and the very survival of the church depend on our obedience to that call. Let me explain.

To Jews and Christians alike Jerusalem has always symbolized the safe stronghold of faith, where the age-long forms of worship are offered. For us Jerusalem is all the traditional centres of our religious observance – the village churches, our great cathedrals, the eucharist shared Sunday after Sunday, the Christmas carols, the Easter flowers, the confirmation class, the wedding bells, new names on the baptismal roll, old names on the war memorial, the PCC and the parish fête. Everything, in fact, that most of us mean by 'the church'. It has to do with home, and coming home. When we talk about 'our church' we don't mean the one we can see from the office window.

That's Jerusalem. And the Risen Christ does meet us there in prayer and sacrament, in the fellowship and the festivals, and his comings give it all an infinite value still. And yet – that was not the way he planned it. He intended something much more vivid for us, something much more workaday and all-inclusive. 'He is going on before you into Galilee; there you will see him.'

Galilee is the secular world, where people are expected to keep religion out of it. The Jews called it 'Galilee of the Gentiles', which literally means 'the international district'. Cosmopolitan Galilee is where the disciples earn their living. It is the commercial arena with a tough code of its own, and it has a history of radical politics. In Jesus' own lifetime the guerilla hero, Judas of Galilee, had led a rising against the foreign government. The people of Jerusalem wanted no connection whatever between Galilee and their idea of Christ. 'What,' they exclaimed, according to St John, 'will Christ appear from Galilee?' Yet that is precisely where he always intended us to find him.

For most people who live outside our great conurbations, home is only one end of the line. For the commuters – the company directors, stockbrokers, members of the Lords or the Commons, civil servants, lawyers – for the seamen, the dock-workers at the container ports, and the hauliers, for the farmers and market gardeners, the other end of the line matters enormously; a great part of life is lived there. And according to the promise of the Risen Christ that is where we can discover for ourselves that he is indeed alive and powerful, and as personally available for us now as he was for his disciples at the beginning of it all. If that were to happen to even a few of us, there would be an end to all our gloomy anxieties about the church and its future. We should need no more conferences about the meaning of mission, for at last we would have found something so surprising we simply couldn't keep it to ourselves.

A friend of mine, a priest who works in London, was invited last March to lead a discussion every Wednesday evening for the six weeks of Lent for the congregation of a church in Surrey. It is what one would call a wealthy parish and most of the men who turned out for those discussions have a job in the City of London. He chose as his theme: 'Christ at both ends of the line'. He showed from a study of the Bible the sort of question that a Jesus who is really alive and at large in the world is bound to be asking about the objectives of a big company and its methods of achieving them, about its responsible use of resources, and of the time of the people it employs. In the middle of the fourth discussion people became so disturbed and angry that their vicar intervened, offering to let them off the hook by taking the two remaining Wednesdays himself. Out of politeness to the guest they declined this offer, but for the last two weeks the discussions were dead because they had all turned in on themselves. The church as a whole still prefers to meet Jesus Christ behind the closed doors of its own weekend Jerusalem, and does not want to find him alive in the Galilee of the job, of politics and of international affairs.

That friend of mine is no provocative hothead. He appreciates the complexity of the problems and certainly won the respect of a group of top executives with whom he took an exacting course at the London Business School. During that course they were one day playing a business game in which each in turn made a make-believe decision to invest or sell or buy out, which was immediately fed into a computer to work out the score, as it were. After one of the others had had his turn my friend asked him out of genuine curiosity: 'As you made that decision, which was uppermost in your mind – increasing the profits, improving the product or benefiting the people?' This was met with a bewildered stare, a long pause, and then the reply: 'I've never once asked myself that question.' Some time later that particular businessman stopped going to church. 'Since that question was put to me,' he said, 'I've had to rethink my whole existence. I feel as if I'm starting again at the beginning. For years I've been attending church. In two places I was a churchwarden. But no-one ever asked me that question in a church, so I reckon I was wasting my time.'

Commerce, industry and the making of wealth are not, of course, the only aspects of the world's life about which Christ's disciples hear him asking such divinely simple questions. In the medical schools and hospital wards he asks, 'What is health?' and, 'What is a human being?' The Christian teacher is the one who is learning to see the whole process of education through Christ's eyes and to ask, 'What are we doing, and why?'

The Christian politician in national or local government is not necessarily the one who takes the predictable line on certain moral issues, but the one who in every decision refuses to pursue narrow, sectional interests, and tries to take the whole view into account because he is serving God's world. Nothing less than that can save us from the epidemic of social irresponsibility which has infected our national life.

It is going to be painfully hard to turn around and run counter to all the assumptions and habits of the working world. It is going to cost more than ordinary courage can bear. And it is precisely at this point that we shall either prove or disprove that Jesus is alive. For we claim not only that he makes us see things in a new light, but that he sets us free to do things in a new way. It is easy enough to recite that in the religious environment of our Jerusalem, but it is in the Galilee of politics, commerce and international affairs that we actually put his resurrection to the test. So this is not a shallow gospel of social reform. I am talking about repentance and faith, forgiveness and salvation, in the critically realistic terms the world understands. It is for the honour of our Saviour that we must go and find him in Galilee.

In my enthusiasm for the living Christ who is waiting to be encountered at the other end of the line, do I seem to undervalue the traditional role of the parish churches at this end? That is not at all my intention. It is in our 'Jerusalem' of Sunday worship and local church fellowship that we re-enact and re-affirm the fundamentals of our faith. In that sense we in our mission, like the apostles in theirs, must begin at Jerusalem. But in another sense Jerusalem comes into her own as the place for celebrating the things that God has done elsewhere. The prayers and confessions at a Sunday eucharist take on a new pungency when they make mention of the difficulties or opportunities facing particular members of the congregation in their weekday world. The praise and thanksgiving are far more vivid when the company of friends rejoices over some breakthrough, some miracle of the Risen Lord, which one of their number has reported from the difficult world of work.

Many of us who have known and loved our Lord for many years in the Jerusalem of our private religious life are in need of a further and deeper conversion to the Christ of Galilee. His promise and his invitation still stand. 'He is going before you into Galilee; there you shall see him.'

23

The Resurrection Life

The resurrection of Jesus came upon his friends like a slow dawning. All the stories emphasized this. Apart from that crowd of over 500 which Paul reports, it was in ones and twos and small groups that they came to believe he was still alive. It was some time before that rising sun banished the heavy mists of fear, despair and disbelief. They frequently had difficulty in recognizing him, but it was recognition which broke upon them in the end.

Once they had grasped the fact that they had actually met him again it became their secret. They could not keep it to themselves, but it was the most impossible secret to shout from the housetops. How could anyone else believe it? There had been no trumpets. An earthquake perhaps, but nothing had changed. The crucifiers were still in power, immovably, with no more than a ridiculous rumour to shake their complacency, a rumour that most of them never even heard.

Whatever 'happened' early that morning while it was still dark, this is the way Easter was experienced. It is still the only way in which Easter is experienced. What happens is that, in ones and twos and small groups, people come to know that Jesus is alive. They cannot prove it. They cannot argue it. They cannot explain it. As far as they are concerened, they do not need to.

They can no longer speak of him in the past tense. He is here and now. Not a memory. Not an influence. Even to say a 'person' is too limiting. The only word that conveys this certainty is 'Lord', and that is impossible to define. To say 'Jesus is alive!' and 'Jesus is Lord!' is to say the same thing. It means that one can address him and be addressed by him in almost the same way as one can speak with God. The living presence one meets in that intercourse is unmistakably Jesus of Nazareth, yet his life seems to radiate in everything and fills the universe. He is alive with an absolute and ultimate life.

But it is still an impossible secret to shout from the housetops. How can anyone else be expected to believe that Jesus is alive if this strange conviction has not grasped him in the same way? The only persuasive evidence that Christians have ever had is the quality of their own fellowship. For the aliveness of Jesus does somehow flow into the strangely fearless, strangely honest, strangely caring and accepting relationship which sometimes and in some places is to be found among Christians. It actually happens far too infrequently, alas, but when it does appear there is nothing else quite like it. It is a very distinct quality of love. It is described in the New Testament; you meet it in some of the stories of the Desert Fathers and frequently among the Celtic saints. It shines out very brightly in the witness of St Francis and his companions. We can all think of moments when we have met it in individuals and communities of our own day.

Even when we fall far short of this pattern we have glimpses of it towards which we strive. And these glimpses, these ideals, are not, as we might expect, different in different cultures any more than they have been different in various periods of history. This special quality of love and aliveness is always recognizable. It is when people see this and are drawn to it that it dawns on them also that Jesus is alive. These are what the present pope so movingly called 'The Easter people'.

But there is something missing from the picture I have drawn. It is all too often missing from the picture of its fellowship which the church tries to draw. And its absence explains why the Easter message, 'Jesus is alive!' leaves so many unconvinced.

What is this 'Lord' worth in face of the big institutions, the big systems, the big interests? What price resurrection, when so many crucifixions are still going on? What are the powerless, the poor and the hungry to hope for amidst the bullying centurions and the trampling legions of the peacekeeping system?

They look for justice and an end to poverty, they hope for liberation and dignity; and the Bible promises these things. The Bible promises them a champion, a conquering messiah, a miracle-working leader. Yet even while the promise stirs them, the truly poor, the real sufferers, are sceptical. The powerless can never fully trust a man of power, even though he comes as liberator, even though he breaks the bands of death. They have seen it all before. Those finest of all freedom fighters, the Maccabees, turned into tyrants in time and were followed by the Herods, with not much to choose between them. When the victims come out on top and the powerless seize power, their representatives take over the big institutions, the big systems, and start to regulate and manipulate as before. No one has much faith in a mighty victor any longer.

It is Thomas, the sceptical saint, who has the answer for these sceptics of our day. They came to Thomas with news of the greatest revolution of all, a new Kingdom, a new creation, and he could not believe. They told him of a man of such power he had conquered even death, and Thomas could not believe. They reported a miracle: they had seen with their own eyes fish and honeycomb eaten by this man who had conquered. And Thomas could not believe.

'You can keep your miracle. Let him show me his wounds. If he has wounds I will believe, but if there are no scars, forget about him, forget about your fish.'

Thomas is the saint who makes sure that the Easter people do not omit the missing factor. He shows what there is in this story of resurrection which we can celebrate without hollow unreality in the midst of these grievous years, in the midst of our powerlessness. Only a Lord with wounds can save us now. To us who are so captive to the principalities and powers liberation wears the face, not of the conquering hero, but of the fellow victim on the cross. When you come to think of it, the first person to bear witness to the *aliveness* of Jesus was the man who was dying at his side and dared to ask for a place in his Kingdom. The real Easter people have the exhausted, enduring faces of Mother Teresa, Helder Camara, and thousands like them. The characteristic actions of the resurrection life are wiping away the tears, showing scars and sharing food.

24

Most Glorious Lord of Life

Easter is the annual celebration of the victory of life over death, of life *through* death. Perhaps nothing is more important than that the church in every place should grasp the significance of this, for the struggle between life and death is going on around us every day. We are not automatically on the side of life. There is a strange gravitational pull towards death. All the easy choices and all the cowardly choices move us in the direction of self-destruction. It takes a deliberate decision to stand on the side of life. 'I have set before you life and death, blessing and curse. Therefore choose life!'

God is in himself the essence of all aliveness. In many books of the Old Testament he is called 'the living God'. He is himself the inexhaustible source, like a hidden artesian well, from which life in all its forms is perpetually flowing, perpetually renewed. 'All that came to be was alive with his life.' In a universe that is issuing from such an indefatigable Creator, death is in truth a transient episode, serving the processes of developing life, like sleep before a new waking up, or like labour before birth. Emily Brontë affirms this in her brave poem, *Last Lines*.

> 'There is no room for Death,
> Nor atom that his might could render void:
> Thou – *Thou* art Being and Breath,
> And what Thou art may never be destroyed.'

Death has become the dark intruder and enemy of life only because something sick and twisted in human nature grew fascinated with death. We seem unable to take our eyes off death. We are literally 'hung up' on death, so that instead of passing through it into life we see it as the end. Our fear gives it substance and vitality (though this is a contradiction in terms), and death becomes something we can take into our own hands and mete out to others. In a manner quite different from the beasts of prey who are innocent in their killing, we are dealers in destruction.

The human race has raised death to the status of a usurping king and set the stage for his age-long conflict with life.

Into that arena came Jesus Christ, 'most glorious Lord of Life'. Into his humanity the aliveness of God flowed pure and complete. If one had to choose one adjective to describe the personality of Jesus it would surely be 'alive'. He moved among his fellows more intensely alive than all of them to the reality of God, more alive to the things that were coming upon the world at that moment in history, more alive to the inner reality of the men and women he encountered, especially those needing recognition and love. The vibrant life that was in him flowed out for others in healing, deliverance and restoration.

Life consists of spontaneous responses. Life moves forward by taking risks and by spending itself totally for the sake of fuller life. While holding consistently to its own pattern, it is always finding new ways around the obstacles in its path. So life is always doing what has never been done before. Life is always unique.

That is exactly what we see in human terms in the person of Jesus. So he was in conflict with all those attitudes which extend the power and dominion of death – the fear of spontaneity which builds its rigid defences of law and tradition; the supreme regard for what is safe, expedient and self-preserving; the mistrust of innovation; the insistence on levelled conformity.

These were the issues between Jesus and his opponents, as the Fourth Gospel makes abundantly clear. The great set-piece of the raising of Lazarus ends with the high-priestly verdict: 'It is expedient that one man should die for the people rather than that the whole nation should perish,' and the climax of the trial before Pilate comes with the words of those same priests: 'We have a law; and by that law he ought to die...' That summed it all up. It still does.

But 'in him was life'. Not the normal brief portion which is our lot, but the inexhaustible source itself, ever rebuffed and frustrated, but ever persisting. 'I am the dance, and the dance goes on.' 'What we have to grasp is not so much that the resurrection happened to Jesus, just as the crucifixion did (though I firmly believe that is true, since our faith is an incarnational faith to the very end), but that he is the resurrection and the life. The great Bishop Westcott says in his commentary on St John: 'He does not say "I promise", or "I procure", or "I bring", but "I am". Life (Resurrection) is present, and this Life is in a Person.'

'Because I live, you will live also.' By putting those words into the mouth of Christ before his death the Fourth Gospel makes them refer to the aliveness of the incarnate Word from the moment of his coming into the world. 'In him was life.' But now, after the death and resurrection, the gift of the Holy Spirit was going to make possible a union of spirit between each Christian and the Risen Christ. The inner being of each one of us is knit with him, we 'dwell in him, and he in us'.

'Because I live, because I *am* life, you shall live also.' The pure aliveness of Jesus of Nazareth had been evidence, if they had only understood, that in him was the source of life which death would never extinguish. What evidence is there that we Christians are partakers of his life and will share his resurrection, unless it be some more intense aliveness in us here and now? Our singing 'We are the Easter people!' will sound convincing only when we look alive and are found to be in conflict with everything that tempts us to choose death.

Today there are many voices enticing people into the ways of death. As in the days of Christ, they speak in tones of prudence, expedience and self-protection. They say, for example, that it would be sensible to have an abortion. Now, I am not among those who would rule out such a decision for every case, but I believe that far more often than not a decision to terminate a pregnancy is a vote against life – not only against the life of the unborn child but, at a profound psychological level, a vote against vitality itself.

I feel the same about our handling of the nuclear deterrent. I have in the past been persuaded by the sincerity and the logic of those who sought to lock up the frightful possibility of mass destruction by making retaliation so inevitable that none would dare to unleash the boomerang. But the argument has shifted its ground. Now the voice of prudence and self-preservation is talking of the deterrent as though it were another weapon that might be used as a 'shot across the bows' of an army preparing to invade and, if used, had best be used first. That we should be the dealers in such destruction is no longer unthinkable. We are caught in the gravitational pull towards death. To stand on the side of life calls for the risks and initiatives of a different policy.

For behind every considered policy there is a bias either towards death or towards life. The arguments or the weapons or the methods you use reveal which side you are on. Was that why Jesus declined Peter's sword and the merciful women's drugged wine?

But aliveness will win, the enduring aliveness of God. Year after year Easter and Pentecost renew the promise that 'in Christ Jesus the life-giving law of the Spirit has set you free from the law of sin and death ... Those who live on the level of our lower nature have their outlook formed by it, and that spells death; but those who live on the level of the Spirit have the spiritual outlook, and that is life and peace.' After every winter the spring flowers are drawn back into the light of the sun. So may we be drawn back from our falling away and up into Christ who is our life and in him grow sensitive to the reality of God, spontaneously responsive to the glory and pain of the world, less prudential in our self-giving, more daring in our risks, each marked with the liveliness and singularity of a child of God.

25

Make Disciples

*'Full authority in heaven and earth has been committed to me. Go therefore
to all nations and make them my disciples.' (Matthew 28.18–19)*

Those words must have brought a stunned surprise to the people who
heard them. They countermanded all the previous instructions Jesus had
given them. 'Do not take the road to Gentile lands,' he had told the
apostles, 'nor enter any Samaritan town, but go rather to the lost sheep of
the house of Israel.' That was in line with his own mission which was just
as rigorously confined. 'I have not been sent to any but the lost sheep of
the house of Israel.' He had apparently remained true to the intention of the
Old Covenant to raise up a holy people in the midst of the other nations.
So the commandment given from that mountain in Galilee sounds like a
total contradiction. And so it was. Never forget that the mission to all nations
flows directly and continuously from the supreme contradiction and reversal
of the resurrection of Jesus. When his tomb was broken open, the exclusive Old Covenant was also broken open, and now our own centralized
old Christendom is being broken open. 'Go therefore, because of that, to
all nations', to the unexpected, the unprecedented, the formerly forbidden. The God of mission is the God of surprises, as Jesus learnt from his
own encounters with non-Jews. Four only are recorded in the Gospels,
and each brought an astonishing contradiction and paradox to light.

The first was the conversation with the Samaritan woman (John 4).
Samaritans were not exactly non-Jews. They were Gentiles in origin who
had adopted a garbled version of Judaism but one so different that true
Jews had no dealings with them and Jesus himself said, 'You worship
without knowledge; we know what it is we worship.' That's why she
was astonished. 'What! You, a Jew, ask for a drink from me, a Samaritan
woman?'

Here was the first great paradox of mission. Those who have some-
thing to teach, something to give, must start by receiving. Knowledge of
God's truth is no just cause for self-sufficiency. Mission is an exchange:
'Give me ... If you knew ... you would ask me and I would give.'

She knew that Jews considered themselves superior, so she imagined that their mission was one of displacement, a matter of either/or. 'This mountain or Jerusalem the right place for the temple.' But Jesus said, 'Neither; but something beyond both. Worshipping the Father in spirit and in truth.'

Next she looks for some common ground – Messiah; they both believe in him. 'When he comes he'll make everything clear.' 'Yes, but that time is now.' Mission is exchange, I talking with you.

Then came the centurion whose servant was racked with the pain of some muscular disease. Jesus offered to come at once, but the soldier stopped him. 'You need only give the order. I can see that because I too am a man under discipline.' He had detected in Jesus the one unmistakeable sign of real authority – obedience. All authority in heaven and on earth was his on the strength of his obedience unto death. This is another paradox of mission. 'I am doing the work of him who sent me' – that was the only warrant Jesus claimed for his actions. So now it was his turn to be astonished, for he had never met with such quick recognition in Judaism or its teachers. They were forever asking, 'By what authority are you doing this? Show your credentials in some miraculous sign.' Yet this pagan could see at a glance that Jesus had received his commission from a higher power, and Jesus for his part recognized this as the gift of faith. Mission entails mutual recognition.

The next Gentile to be encountered was that Phoenician mother down at the coast (Matthew 15). It is the only occasion we know of when Jesus set eyes upon the open sea. Up to this point the Bible tells a land-locked story. The Holy Land was criss-crossed by walls of partition enclosing the inheritance of many different families and clans. The social and moral life of the Chosen People was similarly marked out with lines of distinction and separation. The coastal strip, from Philistine to Roman times, had generally been occupied by idolators. The sea itself was feared as a symbol of lawlessness and chaos.

I can imagine the wonder with which Jesus took in the unbroken expanse of the blue Mediterranean, ships of all nations converging upon the ancient ports of Tyre and Sidon and putting out again with fresh cargoes. Did it perhaps occur to him there that this might be a more favourable setting for the fulfilment of God's promise to Abraham, that through his descendants all people on earth would be blessed? Why else should this Gentile woman's persistent cry for help have aroused in him such a conflict that he put to the disciples his sense of being sent to Israel alone?

It was her wit that resolved the question for him. When he spoke of a meal prepared for children only, she pointed out that a table edge is no perimeter fence, least of all where children are sitting, so even the dogs may expect some over-spill. From now on the sea will flood into what remains of the Bible story. Mission is a free trade area.

The final foretaste of that breakthrough came a few days before the crucifixion, when those 'Greeks' appeared in the temple (John 12). The word indicates that they were not converts to Judaism but Gentiles who came to the festival as sightseers or superstitiously to offer a sacrifice, as Jewish law allowed. This group, however, had another motive: they wanted to meet Jesus.

The great opening up, the fulfilment of God's purpose for all nations, was at hand. But that worldwide mission was to flow out of the resurrection. What it had to bring was not simply news but new life. And there can be no harvest of that crop before life has first been laid down. This is the greatest of all the contradictions at the heart of mission. In order to find new life and in order to bring it to others a dying is required. That was true for the Lord of the harvest; it is also true for the labourers he sends, and the agencies through which he sends them. The paradox stands firm. So does the promise of resurrection.

26

I Am Ascending

*'Go to my brothers and tell them that I am now ascending to my
Father and your Father, to my God and your God.' (John 20.17)*

It is impossible to be absolutely sure what the people who experienced
the coming of the Son of God to the world were able to make of it at
the time. Who did they think he was, when they watched him preaching
and healing in Galilee, when he was captured and killed, or when rumours
of his resurrection began to spread? I don't expect they could have told
you themselves, not with any clarity, for their minds must have been in a
whirl of changing thoughts, and it was all so unexpected. But one thing
must have been clear. When they were with him, God seemed nearer and
more real. When he was taken from them and killed, it was as though
they had lost God. And when they knew him to be alive and ever
present, God was with them again in a way they had never known before,
even during those lovely years in Galilee. Long before they had anything
like a Christian creed, they knew that Jesus and God belonged together
for ever and inseparably. And their way of saying this was, 'He ascended
into heaven.' That was his nature. That was his home.

The Fourth Gospel may have been written last of all, but however it
came to be put together, I am certain that it is putting into words many
of those first basic convictions that formed in the minds of the disciples
through their actual experience of Jesus. It is perfectly summed up in
those promises ascribed to him in the Great Discourse before his death.
'I will not leave you bereft. I am coming back to you. In a little while the
world will see me no longer, but you will see me. Because I am alive, you
will be alive too, and then you will know that I am in the Father and you
in me and I in you.' That isn't theology. That is the burning material of
experience, which will crystallize into theology later on.

And so the phrase that is put into the mouth of Jesus in those discourses
before his death several times over is, 'I am going to the Father.' That is
what we celebrate on Ascension Day. 'I am going to the Father.' 'I came
from the Father and have come into the world. Now I am leaving the

world and going to the Father. He who has faith in me will do what I am doing, he will do greater things still, because I am going to the Father.'

The ascension of Jesus Christ into heaven does not separate him from us; rather, it involves us with him in the same destiny and the same way. 'He who has faith in me will do what I am doing' – that is, going to the Father. For though he left the world, he did not leave his human nature. There is humanity in heaven now. This is the extraordinary thing which we are compelled to affirm again and again on this great festival. Humanity itself has been taken up into God. As the Fourth Gospel portrayed it at the very beginning, 'Do you believe because I said I saw you under the fig tree? I tell you, you shall see the angels ascending and descending upon the Son of Man.' The ladder of Jacob's dream is now open to all of us in a constant to and fro access with heaven itself. There is no barrier now between earth and heaven. Because of that it is possible for his will to be done on earth as it is in heaven, and Ascension Day challenges us to ascend in heart and mind, yes, even in our bodily action, where he has gone before. 'I have gone to prepare a place for you. In my Father's house there are many stopping places, and at each point along the road, I have gone before, preparing it for you, so that where I am, there you may be also.'

'Go and tell my brothers, I am now ascending to my Father and *your* Father, to my God and *your* God,' for your relationship is to be the same now, 'that where I am, you may be also.' I have taken humanity into the Godhead – *there* is your place, which I have gone to prepare for you. Live in God and let the life of God live in you, and refuse the old idea that heaven is distant from the life of this world, for it is no longer. The barriers have all been broken down.

But this going to the Father refers to everything that happens to Jesus from the moment of his going forth from the Upper Room until his taking up into heaven. In the high priestly prayer, he prayed: 'I am to stay no longer in the world. But they are still in the world, and I am on my way to thee.' And in the words he spoke to Mary Magdalene in the resurrection garden, he still says, 'I have not yet ascended, but go and tell my brothers I am now ascending to my Father and your Father, my God and your God.' Death and burial and resurrection and ascension are all one movement, the going to the Father, the being with God. And so that same Fourth Gospel marvellously uses the words *lifted up* about his death and about his resurrection and about his ascension. For it is all one movement, lifted up, but only through self-sacrifice, self-giving, self-oblation, the dying into life, the being lifted up, that all may believe.

And that is the place that he is preparing for us. 'Where I am, you cannot come now, but you shall come hereafter.' 'Oh,' says Peter, 'no, I want to come straight away!' He understood what he was talking about. 'I will lay down my life for you.' 'Yes, Peter, that is what I am talking about, that is the place I am preparing for you. But before the cock crows tonight, you will have denied me three times. You are not ready yet. But you will come hereafter.' Into death, into resurrection, into oneness with God – you will go to the Father as I am going to the Father. 'Where I am, there you may be also. The way, you know.' There is no escaping that way, that is the way of going to the Father. But there is no stopping that way either, for if we go forward, the only end will be heaven.

'Go, tell my brothers, I am now ascending to my Father and *your* Father, my God and *your* God. The place I prepare is a place for *you*.'

27

There is a Man in Heaven

Those few who shared the secret that Jesus Christ was not dead but alive were growing accustomed to the experience of what appeared to be his comings and goings. Perhaps it was simply that their minds were becoming adjusted to the fact of his aliveness, and taking in more of the nature of his presence. Yet to put it that way makes it sound too subjective, whereas I personally am convinced that their growing realization was forced upon them on each occasion by an actual happened-ness, of which Jesus was the activator, not the object.

At any moment he might be there, but in particular he would be there for those who were in need of him – for the desperate woman in the garden, for Peter in his remorse, for the bewildered couple on their way home in the evening, for Thomas in his demand to see for himself. Availability had always been his characteristic, and now his availability seemed to have become universal.

When he came it was as though he had been there all the time, and knew what had been happening to them. And when he left there might be some tangible evidence of his passing – a fire still burning on the shore, a loaf lying in pieces on the table – as though he acknowledged that 'presence' must always be in some sense physical, just as we acknowledge it at any communion service. For, as a rather lovely song puts it, 'Eight crumbs on the table are worth more than all your letters.'

And now that they had become sure of him he gave them this culminating disclosure which we call the ascension, after which they needed no more such comings save a last unimaginable one to which they would always look forward. 'He was lifted up into heaven,' says Luke. And where was that? Not a withdrawal into another place, but an enlargement out of here into everywhere, out of now into always. The particular Jesus of Nazareth was seen to be the universal Christ. 'Where is he now?' asks Pilate's wife in John Manfield's play. 'Let loose in the world, madam,' replies the centurion, 'where neither Jew nor Roman can stop the truth.' That availability of his love, which had been stretched beyond human limit in Galilee and Jerusalem, had now become limitless. He would always be there for everyone.

Luke, who is the one who tells the story of Ascension Day, sees it as the second half of a double movement. In his account of the Transfiguration of Jesus he says that Jesus' mystical conversation with Moses and Elijah was about 'his Exodus which he should accomplish in Jerusalem'. Remember the Exodus out of Egypt was a going up into the wide freedom of a promised land. That is how Jesus spoke of what was going to happen in Jerusalem. And immediately afterwards Luke's Gospel sets the beginning of the long progress up to Jerusalem which he describes with the word 'ascended'. 'He went on, ascending to Jerusalem', to the hill called Golgotha, and thence to the total availability of resurrection life. That was the full measure of his Exodus into freedom.

The way of ascension passes through the cross. Total availability costs not less than death. Presence, really to be present to another, involves a complete self-giving. Bread must be broken in order to be shared.

So no-one can ascend who will not first descend. It is the ancient truth of Persephone and the corn goddess. 'A grain of wheat remains a solitary grain unless it falls into the ground and dies.' Ascension implies incarnation – not apotheosis but a return. 'Now the word ascended implies that he also descended to the lowest level, down to the very earth' (Ephesians 4.9).

'He did not think to snatch at equality with God, but made himself nothing, assuming the nature of a slave. Bearing the human likeness, revealed in human shape, he humbled himself, and in obedience accepted even death, death on a cross. Therefore God raised him to the heights and bestowed on him the name above all names, that at the name of Jesus every knee should bow – in heaven, on earth and in the depths – and every tongue confess, "Jesus Christ is Lord", to the glory of God the Father' (Philippians 2.6–11).

So that he might fill the universe the Christ was emptied to the last drop of self.

But in his ascended glory he remains man. Dare we believe that? If incarnation did something to God, ascension did something to matter. This was the culmination of the stupendous process we call creation. The God who went to such infinite pains in the making and development of electronic systems, molecules, and chemicals, metals, rocks and living cells, structured forms and responsive nerves, did not at the final stage abandon matter; he liberated it. We have too closed a view of matter. Its potential is far more open-ended than we imagine. Consider our new understanding of matter as energy. Consider how consciousness, mind and spiritual awareness have emerged out of matter, transcending it but not leaving it behind.

The ascension of Christ promises the transfiguration of matter, its divinization, as the Orthodox Churches have never ceased to teach. The physical will glow with God like metal enveloped and permeated by fire. 'The universe itself is to be freed from the shackles of mortality and enter upon the liberty and splendour of the children of God' (Romans 8.21). That is the end to which we aspire. And the way is the way of descent, the way of the death of self, again and again, the way of the broken bread shared with all, of the scarred hands that hold the world.

PART FIVE

The New Age

There was a man, surpassingly alive,
whose own truth blazed with such authority
as made the simple and the poor derive
all faith from his and, seeing the road he trod,
they had no heart for any other god.

28

Dare We Be Christians?

Did Jesus Christ found a church? That is certainly the way it has been taught and I have heard speeches in the General Synod of the Church of England that suggest that a major concern of his Galilean ministry was running an ordination training course with an intake of 12 candidates! But on the face of it this seems unlikely. His urgent message was the Kingdom. 'The Kingdom of God is breaking through.' That meant the end of the world as they knew it, with its institutions and its soiled history and its corrupt structures of power. The Kingdom was the gift of a new age, a new dimension; a fulfilment of the past, yes, but so radical it would be like a new birth. And for Jesus the supreme manifestation of the new age, its essential quality, was a new relationship with God. This was the new wine that could not be contained in old wineskins without bursting them.

'The Kingdom is at hand' meant *God* is at hand, so near that anyone who will turn to face him may know him with the certainty and intimacy of direct knowledge, without mediation of teachers, tradition or church. 'The Kingdom of God is within you, among you, come with power.' They could see that he knew what he was talking about since all his actions sprang from just such an intimacy with God. The life of the Kingdom as he lived it out was a reflection of the character of the Father, and this was to be the way for them all.

Then came his death and resurrection. Against all likelihood a few of them, that small inner circle of women and apostles, found that he was alive. 'He appeared' was how they put it, and the experience was repeated on different occasions, often enough to seal an entirely new kind of relationship between them and him. He became an abiding presence – 'I am with you always to the end of time.'

But he was also one with God. That intense intimacy they had seen in his relationship with the heavenly Father was now recognized by them as having the same kind of permanence as his presence with them. 'He was taken into heaven' was how they put it. There was a oneness between Jesus and God that was more than closeness. But at the same time there was oneness more than closeness between the Risen Christ and themselves.

It must have taken some years of the growing fellowship life to crystallize this experience of his oneness with them. Of course they associated it with the experience of Holy Spirit in their fellowship life. This powerful aliveness was God in the midst of them; it was the Risen Lord still present. The Spirit was Spirit of God, Spirit of Jesus.

But while they spoke of Spirit they were at pains to emphasize an almost physical quality in the abiding presence of Christ in their fellowship which was not fully expressed in talk about the Spirit. The constant breaking of the bread in their house meetings in obedience to his command must have enhanced this sense of bodily contact in their union with him, and may also have become necessary as an expression of that sense. At any rate, reference to the body of the Lord continued to be an element in the experience of his presence in their midst which they could not abandon.

Within about 25 years of the death of Jesus, Paul at least, if not others, had formulated this by saying that the Christian fellowship is the risen body of Christ, and that the individual Christian is *in* Christ. He means this quite literally, for he took bodies more seriously than we do. In Paul's view, and that of most Jewish people of the time, a person's body is himself. A person is not *in* his body; he does not *have* body; he *is* his body.

So when these first Christians take as basic the humanity of Jesus, even though they have not known him in the flesh, and then believe that he is alive and at large in the universe and forever present with them, they cannot 'disembody' their thought of him, for he, in common with all humanity, is his body still. This insight lies behind the emphasis on the resurrection of the body, first of the Risen Christ and then of our own anticipated resurrection.

So, in speaking of the church as the body of Christ and of each Christian as being *in* Christ, Paul is making very specific that experience of oneness with the ever-present Risen Lord which the original group had had from the beginning. Their fellowship of faith and hope and love, continuing through time, is Christ in the world. The words in the Fourth Gospel gather it all up in perfect simplicity: 'As thou, Father, art in me, and I in thee, so also may they be in us … I in them and thou in me, may they be perfectly one.'

But – and this is the ever-excruciating 'but' which all Christians have to live with – but the church as we have known it could scarcely look less like Jesus Christ alive and at large in the world. Was he ever boring to the young, captive to tradition? Was his welcome limited to people of a certain sort, or were there any with whom he could not eat and drink? Was he worried over declining numbers or falling income? Was he bent on securing his survival and afraid of taking risks?

Oh, I know it is easy and cheap to deride the institutional churches. It is tempting to give vent to one's disappointment over oneself by castigating the fellowship as a whole, and ignoring the saints in its midst and all the quiet achievements. We should at least have enough intelligence and sense of history to realize that, simply because the world did not come to an end 2000 years ago, the church was bound to become, among other things, an institution. Any 'system' is a structure to ensure the continuity and communication of a particular identity or idea. Had the church relied only upon local spontaneity it would long ago have lost all coherence and its message would have become infinitely more fragmented and contradictory than it is now, and that is saying a good deal. No movement can sustain the simplicity of the first generation. For one thing a second generation faces questions and moral decisions that never troubled the first. When apostles have died out, Christians need agreed guidelines to deal with as many contingencies as they can foresee.

Where we do have to challenge the institution is where it is actually standing for the opposite of what it seeks to communicate and has become an obstacle to people's faith in its message. How can people hear what we *say* when what we *are* is thundering in their ears? We cannot proclaim the astonishing unconditional love and acceptance of God, revealed in Jesus, while we are selective, discriminating or exclusive in our treatment of fellow Christians or of anyone else. We cannot open people's eyes to the vision of a God whose hands are tied by love, revealed in the cross of Christ, while we set up a power structure of our own among the other power structures. We cannot preach a gospel for the poor unless we share God's bias towards them. We cannot heal without opening ourselves to the flow of healing in a constantly forgiven and forgiving community.

Dare we become Christian? Dare we face and accept God in his reality of suffering, inexhaustible love as he has been revealed in Jesus? Dare we change into the people of *that* God? Every Easter confronts us with a stone that has to be rolled away.

29

Christian Mission in an Age of Violence

I think that we are moving into a much more turbulent and violent period than we have been used to. In one sense, human creatures have always been violent and it might be argued that things we regarded in recent years as very exceptional are becoming much more commonplace and almost taken for granted.

It is not only in Britain or in the United States that people are aware of the horror of the amount of violence there is around, but in almost every country there is a situation of deep division of one sort or another. Violence is all the way round, so that the shots and explosions which we are becoming used to are, in a sense, only an indication of the world in which we have to bear our witness – and not just bear our witness but try to find out what it means to be engaged in the ministry of reconciliation.

What are the springs of violence?

I suggest that a good deal of it can be explained simply by the fact of the steadily increasing stress under which we are living: stress due to increased speed and to the amount of noise that surrounds more and more human beings; stress of numbers, the sheer pressure of population. We know that animals, when they are crowded together in a narrow space with no outlet, show neurosis and ferocious fighting amongst one another simply as a result of overcrowding.

The communication explosion is, I think, another of the sources of violence. Whether it is television or newspapers or radio, we are making one another more aware of disturbing things happening in other parts of the world which previous generations would not have heard of. Disturbance comes pouring into our lives and is doubly disturbing because we can do nothing about it. The less opportunity we have for an active reaction to it the more we store up our fear inwardly, and this adds again to the stress.

Closely allied with stress is the condition called 'exposure'. Because everything is changing so quickly, most human beings today feel that the old shell has been stripped from them, and there they are, isolated in their individualism, with a menacing world all around, and nothing but their own devices to fall back on. Mobility creates this exposure. People move from one address to another, from one job to another, so quickly that they are continually having to go through the experience of being a stranger.

A more subtle cause of violence is parental irresponsibility. I am thinking of the generation which became parents during or just after the Second World War. I think we were a generation that was peculiarly afraid of dying. It may have had something to do with living through that war, it may have had even more to do with the catching up on us of the general loss of religious faith. We were so afraid of dying that we were afraid of even being middle-aged. Consequently that generation of parents refused to bear the anxieties of middle-age, and projected its own anxieties onto its children. So instead of setting the boundaries, taking a normal parent's responsibility for the 'house rules' of a home, and suffering the occasional hostility that is the price of any responsibility, my generation lost their nerve. They did not want to bear the anxiety of making the decisions and so left their children to make their own and bear the anxiety of it themselves.

So because the children were bearing an anxiety that ought to have been borne by others, they finally built up such stress that it emerged in violence. The most exposed of all, the children of the so-called working class, were the first to become violent. So we got the mods and rockers, Hells Angels, bovver boots, and successive types of vicious hooliganism. Middle-class youngsters followed a little later with a more introverted sort of violence against the self in the form of drugs and the rash driving of vehicles, as though they were unconsciously hell-bent on destroying themselves. Finally, at the university level, what started as responsible attempts to bear the great issues of the world became less and less responsible, and led to more conflict with the police than in the early days.

You may disagree with this analysis and suggest other reasons for the existence of violence, but the fact that it is there and is one of the most urgent challenges to our Christian mission, is, I think, inescapable.

What is Christian mission in a violent situation?

Remember that the civilization that could crucify Jesus also crucified people by the tens of thousands. It was the civilization that had Roman games for its entertainment. It was a very violent age. And in that age Paul again and again speaks of Christian witness in terms of reconciliation.

I think there is a lesson to be learned here. We shall find the right language for talking about the human relation to God by finding the most essential concern within the human family. Take your metaphor from the paramount secular need and let it be a metaphor of men and women's relation to God. Then the whole need, the vertical and the horizontal, will come together as one.

So in that violent age, writing to one of the more violent cities, Corinth, Paul has this great passage: 'From first to last this has been the work of God. He has reconciled us men to himself through Christ, and he has enlisted us in this service of reconciliation.' There you have the vertical and the horizontal. He reconciles us to himself and says, 'Now you know about reconciliation, go and reconcile man with man, faction with faction, and all the other divisions in this city'. Be reconcilers because you have found the ultimate source of reconciliation and the process by which reconcilation works. 'What I mean is, that God was in Christ reconciling the world to himself, no longer holding men's misdeeds against them, and that he has entrusted us with the message of reconciliation.'

Just as we have found the way of using our need for health as a valid means of proclaiming the wholeness that Christ would offer; just as we have used our need for enlightenment and found in the education process a sphere of mission; just as more recently we have gone into the social services and discovered there a way of bringing Christ to human beings; so I think a new sphere of mission is waiting to be discovered in the exercise of deliberate, skilled reconciliation.

In this connection the seventh chapter of John's Gospel excited me the other day because as I read it, it struck me that here we have Jesus at work reconciling, though it does not look like reconciliation. It is a chapter of total hostility. There are four points here that are well worth noting.

First of all Jesus says, 'Whoever has the will to do the will of God shall know whether my teaching comes from him or is merely my own.' He was facing an angry audience that was deeply divided in itself. There were Jews who believed in him but at that moment were no longer able to go along with him. There were those who did not believe in him and were prepared to excommunicate the ones who did. There were the Pharisees waiting for their chance. These could easily be set one against the other. But instead of aligning himself with any one of those groups Jesus starts by saying, 'Whoever wills to do the will of God.' He shows that if you are out for reconciliation, you start by emphasizing a common will for good. If there is to be reconciliation in Northern Ireland or the Middle East it has got to start by bringing together the bits of goodwill wherever they are to be found. That is what we can build on. 'Whoever has the will to do the will of God' is a tremendous starting point.

The second step which Jesus takes is to expose the unacknowledged anger. Suddenly into the middle of this conversation Jesus drops the appalling words, 'Why are you trying to kill me?' The crowd answers, 'You must be mad. Who wants to kill you?' And you can imagine Jesus saying, 'Now come off it. Let's bring this into the open. You do want to kill me, you're that angry with me, aren't you?' Until the unacknowledged anger is brought into the open we are just make-believe reconcilers. This is what Christians are so bad at, because we have this long tradition that Jesus was very nice and we must all be nice too. But Jesus talks about truth and love, not niceness. And the ministry of reconciliation must work for the moment when the real anger breaks surface. It will be a very violent moment and one which we may justly fear, but until we pass through that moment we are nowhere near reconciliation.

The third point may be the hardest of all. You see, something has got to happen to the hostility. Just bringing it into the open does not finish it. It has to go somewhere. I think that is the main message of the perplexing and rather horrifying story about the pigs and the Gaderene maniac. An evil spirit has to go somewhere. I think Jesus' way is to say, 'All right, let it come to me.'

This is the essential truth of the cross. Jesus absorbed into himself the concentrated impact of the world's evil. He was already beginning to do this at the time of this encounter in John's Gospel. Everybody realized that there was tremendous hostility towards Jesus. So they had not expected him to show up publicly at this festival in Jerusalem. But when it was already half over Jesus went up to the temple and began to teach. This was one of those great moments when he laid himself bare to all the hostility that was there. This, in a sense, was the beginning of his passion. In John 7.26 we read that the Jews said, 'Here he is speaking openly.' And they had not a word to say to him. In all this conversation he is the only one who speaks openly. He keeps on telling the awful, bare truth without any tact. They are evasive in everything they say. They don't really want to have a showdown with him, if only he will compromise and let them get away with half truths. But he came to save men and women, and only truth can save. He came to reconcile so he could not let them be with hidden anger. So he has to be open, and he becomes not just a target but a magnet that draws out the hostility until it is focused on him.

The fourth point is that in a situation of this kind we have to proclaim the transcendence of God. We have to say, 'God is above these divisions and these arguments.' So in John 7.28 we see Jesus turning everybody's attention to God. 'I have not come of my own accord. I was sent by the one who truly is, and him you do not know.' This means if we really proclaim the transcendence of God we have to give up identifying him with our ideas of what is right and wrong in the situation. In a situation of conflict, the God-believers always try and identify one side of the conflict as being more in accordance with God's will than the other. This only exacerbates the problem and there is no escape until at last we are willing to set our eyes upon a God who is above our ideas of right and wrong.

At a conference some years ago I put the question: 'Where do you think you can hear the voice of God in Northern Ireland today?' The answers were terribly predictable. 'We can hear the voice of God wherever we see Christians from both sides meeting and talking.' 'We can hear the voice of God in the continual prayer for peace that goes up from all around the world.' One after another they produced instances that obviously in their eyes were good and they identified those with the voice of God. Then I asked what Amos would have said if we had asked him the same question? Is it possible that he would have heard the voice of God in the crash of falling masonry and the crackle of flames? That is what he said in his own day to Israel. God was acting in these terrible events of history, but it was God, and it had nothing to do with their ideas of right and wrong. In fact the prophets were continually saying, 'We have to draw our ideas of right and wrong from God and not argue God from our concept of ethics.' It is the other way round. We have continually to be revising our concept of right and wrong by the immediacy of our experiences of the living God. At those moments we are aware only of him. Afterwards we may find we understand goodness more truly and see better what beauty is. God comes first and that is his transcendence. He must transcend the ideas of right and wrong which are in fact the very things that divide us in these conflicts.

Most of us do not have to live under the bitter history of Ireland or in the multi-racial tension of inner-city areas. Yet, sooner than we expect, we are going to find ourselves reacting to the violence of our times, and if we are not consciously committed to the way of reconciliation, our blindly respectable reactions will be part of the violence. It could be a very extreme part, as it was in Germany when Hitler relied on respectable reactions to bring him to power. So, while we have time, let us learn to practise the ministry of reconciliation in small things, which means taking responsibility when relations are breaking down. Even that will prove to be quite costly.

30

Where Two or Three are Gathered

'Who do people say that I am?' It is interesting that Jesus started with that question because it is the first question that has to be put to the church. It isn't enough to go around proclaiming what we think about Jesus unless we have first discovered what the world is saying about him. If we don't listen to the way they are putting it, if we don't really listen to the underlying wistfulness, lostness, if we simply remain scared of a world that seems to be saying the wrong things about Jesus, then we haven't a chance of being listened to when we say what we think about him.

'Who do people say that I am?' is still a live question, and there are still a great variety of answers, and some of those answers are perplexing to us. They shake our own faith and we have to endure that shaking if we are to be any use at all in proclaiming what we believe is the truth. It always will be a question surrounding us – 'Who do people say that I am?' Listen to what is being written, listen to the radio, listen to Tom, Dick and Harry, listen ...! 'Who do people say that I am?'

And then, turning to them, comes the challenge, 'Who do *you* say that I am?' For it has to be a personal conviction, and not all of us will say it in the same way. The creed isn't enough. It must be *my* creed, *my* way of putting it, and we have to be honest about it. But it has to be a personal conviction, because, as Jesus said to Peter, it isn't a truth that you can learn from other people, it isn't a truth to be learned from mortal man, mortal man cannot give it to us – not to you, not to me, not to the other person. There has to be recognition. Then comes the answer bursting forth, almost before you realize that you believe it, 'But you are the Christ!' or whatever it is that you can say from your own strange conviction.

Where does that conviction come from? It comes from revelation. 'It isn't flesh and blood that gives it to you, but my Father' (Matthew 16.17). And how does my Father give the truth to you? Well, how did he give the truth to the world? By sending a man. Flesh and blood doesn't reveal it to you, but only my Father speaking through flesh and blood, speaking through a human life, speaking through other human lives today, speaking through the actions, not just the words, of a church. As St James says, 'It isn't what you say that conveys your faith to other people, but what you do, your good works,' your behaviour, which actually proclaims the truth in a way that will bring conviction to others.

It is strange that St Mark, who we think probably represents most closely what Peter was teaching as an apostle, especially the story as he told it to new converts and those who were preparing to be baptized, does not in his Gospel report the next bit of the story. But I want to include it nonetheless, so we turn again to St Matthew, who is very good on Peter. It was in response to Peter's recognition, 'You are the Christ', that Jesus went on to say, 'You are Peter, the rock, and on that rock I am going to build my church' (Matthew 16.18).

I have to ask which matters to us most, the rock, or the church that Jesus built on it? You can't confuse the two. The rock is only just the firm bit on which you can actually start to build a church. After that, what people see is the church. The rock is out of sight. Unfortunately the rock falls for the temptation over and over again of an extraordinary pretentiousness. It is the pretentiousness of anybody with leadership or power within the church that has let us down over and over again.

Yes, I know I speak like a Protestant, but there is that much truth in our Protestantism, and we have to watch our church lest we somehow beguile bishops into thinking that they are the ones that have to be seen. If they are true to St Peter, they ought to be out of sight. What matters is the church, the whole body, which grows out of that faith, and they are there to foster it and to guard it, but not to be the point of everybody's attention. But I will give to you who are leaders, who have responsibility, the keys of the Kingdom of God, so that what you open will be opened eternally and what you shut will be shut eternally, what you allow will be allowed even by heaven and what you forbid will be forbidden even by heaven. It is an awesome responsibility.

No wonder Peter felt pretty chuffed, no wonder he began to be a few inches higher when that had been said to him. We do have our great ups when God lifts us up and we think, 'My word, how wonderful to have seen that, how wonderful to be given this degree of responsibility by God.' But there are probably twice as many downs as there are ups, and that is what happened to Peter next.

Now we go back to St Mark, who says, immediately after Peter's recognition of Jesus: 'Taking Jesus aside' – because Jesus had gone on to explain what sort of Messiah he was, and that those who follow must be prepared to follow that kind of Messiah and that was the bit that Peter couldn't take – 'Taking Jesus aside,' Peter remonstrates with him (Mark 8.32). 'You've got it wrong, you don't understand messiahship, dreadful things like that can't happen to messiahs.' The Gospel goes on: 'Jesus, catching sight of the disciples' – there was the church that was beginning to be built on that rock, and that church mustn't listen to what Peter has just said, so Jesus turns, having seen the church, and says, 'Stand behind me, Satan,' that is not what has to be listened to, because that isn't how God thinks, it is how you men think, and I don't want the church to hear that. The church must be protected from Peter, protected from every pretentious coward, mustn't hear his gospel of immunity from suffering or from failure. 'Your thoughts are not my thoughts, saith the Lord, neither are your ways my ways.' It is an ancient thought.

This up and down of the Christian life continues over and over again, and we ought not to be too abased when we make fools of ourselves and get it wrong. We should just learn from that. Neither should we be too elated when once in a blue moon we get it right and the Lord approves and justifies what we have said or what we have been. We need to have an even keel, we need not to take ourselves too seriously. And what safeguard have we got for this awful up and down of pride and abasement? How can we have an even keel?

Every gift of leadership or of insight or of responsibility is meant to be delegated. Others must be trained to share it. In the Christian church, no leader should ever be isolated from the body, just as the rock cannot be separated from the church that is built around it and upon it. It becomes integrated with the whole, and the rockness, the firmness of the rock has to be given to the whole building. Whatever insight, whatever gift any leader, however small, however out of sight, may have received is going to be a threat, is going to be a danger to that person unless he or she immediately sets about delegating. 'Who can I share this with? Who will do this with us?' And so only three chapters after St Matthew has told the story of Peter being given the keys, he refers to that same giving of the keys, but this time it is immediately to *all* the apostles. Even the gift of the keys is shared, even the authority to shut up or to set free, to allow or to forbid. For in chapter 18 Matthew says, after the passage about the church's pastoral care of its difficult members, 'Whatever you forbid on earth shall be forbidden in heaven, whatever you allow on earth shall be allowed in heaven.' And he goes on to say, 'Why should this be so? Why should you have such incredible, awesome authority? I'll tell you.

Wherever two or three are gathered together in my name, I am in the midst.' That is where the authority comes. He didn't say wherever two or three bishops are gathered together in my name; he didn't even say where two or three clergy are gathered together in my name. He said, wherever two or three are gathered together in my name, you have the keys of the Kingdom, you have that tremendous responsibility because it has been delegated. It is the body that matters, not the individual person, and it is to the body that Christ gives his everlasting presence.

31

Who Am I?

*'There was a man, sent by God; his name was John ... he was not
the light, only a witness to speak for the light.' (John 1.6, 8)*

'There was a man ...' – and what a man! 'Verily, I say unto you, among
them that are born of women there hath not risen a greater than John
the Baptist.' In his stripped and sinewy strength, his eagle vision, his mag-
netic attraction, his passionate courage, there was a man. His name was
John. And how emphatically it had been affirmed. The whole strange
story of that nativity is focused upon the *name* of the child. And to the
Jewish people the name establishes the identity. John knew who he was.

That is the first requirement for anyone who is called and sent. If you
have not learned to know yourself, you have not begun to know the
gospel. If you do not possess yourself, you have no self to give and spend
for others. If you are unsure of yourself, you will never support the burden of other selves. If you will not accept yourself, you are bound to
reject others.

How then can we overcome the undermining uncertainty about ourselves, and escape the nagging question, Who am I? By recognizing the
fact that selfhood is never achieved: it is given. We do not name ourselves:
we are named. 'Thou shalt call his name John.' It is God who affirms the
identity of those he calls. It is God who has accepted them in order that
they may accept themselves. Just as in confirmation it is the identity of a
man or woman or child which is being confirmed, so in ordination it is
a person's true selfhood that is being called and called out.

Apostolic ministry begins with the gift of the name. 'So he appointed
the Twelve: to Simon he gave the name Peter; then came the sons of
Zebedee to whom he gave the name Boanerges.' Mark, reflecting Peter's
experience of that ordination, tells how it was accomplished by the giving of names. It seems that Jesus' love of giving his chosen name to each
of his friends was applied to others also. Thomas was called The Twin,
Lebbaeus was nicknamed Thaddaeus, which means 'chesty' – perhaps he
was a more than usually broad-shouldered fisherman!

Spend time enough in the friendship of Christ, and let that silent intimacy give you your identity. Let his knowledge of you deepen your self-knowledge, let his acceptance of you restore your acceptance of yourself, let his quiet 'I am' enable you also to say 'I am'.

But when God has given anyone this precious gift of self-assurance he immediately goes on to teach him to say 'I am not.'

This is the testimony which John gave. When the Jews of Jerusalem sent a deputation of priests and Levites to ask him who he was, he confessed without reserve and avowed: I am not the Messiah.

'What then, are you Elijah?'

'I am not.'

'Are you the prophet we await?'

'No.'

'Then, who are you? We must give an answer to those who sent us. What account do you give of yourself?'

'I am a voice crying in the wilderness, Make the Lord's highway straight.'

The wilderness was itself a symbol of negation. The wilderness is a landscape with no form, no identity, no centre. Sooner or later we all experience the frightening loss of identity which may come upon us in what John Bunyan called 'the wilderness of the world'. Or it may be in the wilderness of the concrete city. For those who, like John, have grown to love the free empty spaces of the desert, it may be the more appalling wilderness of a narrow dungeon of limitation and disappointment. Or men or women may grow sick in heart as they see what happens to other human beings in the wilderness of a society totally absorbed in wage-earning and consumption. And very often the outward desolation is simply the environment that is bound to grow out of the wilderness in our hearts.

In the wilderness people lose their way because there is no way, no boundaries, no centre. People are too far apart for one to be able to point out a direction to another. But a voice suddenly calling in the emptiness gives a centre and a point to which all the meaningless distances can be related. Nothing else than that is required of John. He does not have to have a striking face or a striking personality; he has only to be a voice. A voice calling to men and women on behalf of God, and crying out for God on behalf of them.

'I am not.' That was John's wilderness. The wilderness of not being, of being nothing but a voice in order that another might have substance. 'He must increase, I must decrease.' The friend of the bridegroom who rejoices when all eyes are turned towards the bridegroom, when he sees his own disciples slip away one by one to join the new Master.

The way of ministry is the way of self-naughting, with no trace of self-pity. 'I am not.' The power of the apostle is the power of the zero, the power of being nothing. It is a very great power. One and 12 naughts is a million million.

'I am. I am not.' John is enabled to say both those things, and the call to the ordained ministry is a call to say both those things. It is by saying both those things that we are able to stand for God, because the essential mystery of God's nature is best summed up in the words, 'I am. I am not.' So the Hindu mystic addresses God, saying, 'This art thou and this thou art not.'

So, and only so, can those who are ordained fulfil their task of proclaiming the 'not yet' in the midst of the 'now'. To call men and women to live the life of the future in the present. 'There stands one among you whom you know not, one who is coming.' He is, but he is not yet. The Kingdom is here, and the Kingdom is still to come.

The church in this century has become too anxious about the so-called relevance of its message. We have started to play too many tricks in an attempt to prove our relevance. But what could be more irrelevant than that which is not yet? What could be more irrelevant for John the Baptist as he begins to despair in his dungeon than the message that Jesus returned in answer to his question? Now, if ever, John wants his own identity confirmed; but Jesus does not confirm it. He does not say, 'Tell John he is a prophet and more than a prophet.' He did not say, 'Tell John that among them that are born of women there is none greater than he.' What Jesus said was, 'Tell John how the blind receive their sight, the lame walk, the deaf hear, the dead are raised to life and the poor are hearing the good news' – all the items, in fact, from that prophecy of Isaiah which Jesus had quoted in the synagogue at Nazareth, all the items except the one which was relevant for John. Jesus omitted the phrase about the release of captives. For John the word was still 'Not yet'. It was still 'I am not.'

So in our ministry the passion to get visible results is misdirected. Our eyes should be set on the things that are not, for we deal with a God who calls the things that are not as though they were (Romans 4.17), and who has chosen the things that are not to bring to naught the things that are (1 Corinthians 1.28). If we are to be true to the gospel we must never relax the tension of this paradox of a Kingdom which is and is not yet.

So may the God of hope fill you with all joy and peace in believing, that you may abound in hope in the power of the Holy Spirit.

32

Orders to Serve

I want to share with you some of my thoughts about the real function of the ordained ministry and some new distinctions which we may need to make in future between the three 'orders' of bishops, priests and deacons.

I do not expect to see these changes come with a rush. Most of what follows is an indication of the direction in which I am sure we are going to have to move. But major changes of one sort or another are bound to come, if only because so many aspects of our society are undergoing profound and very rapid change, just as much in the country as in the towns. If the patterns of our church organization were not changing also to match the new patterns of human society all around us we would have reason to fear, if not for our survival, then certainly for the effectiveness of our mission. We should take heart from the knowledge that the forms of church organization that are familiar to us may be many centuries old, but they are not the only shape which the church has taken in the whole of its history, nor is God limited to those familiar forms for the future that is now unfolding before us.

The first thing I have to say about the function of the ordained ministry is that from now on every ordained person should think of himself or herself primarily as an enabler of groups of ordinary Christians acting together. In the formal worship of the church, even in those functions that are reserved to him or her as an ordained person, the priest is there to enable others to offer the sacrifice of praise and thanksgiving in spirit and in truth. The pastoral ministry is exercised to enable others to discover together the full meaning of their discipleship in the world.

And this understanding of the ordained ministry is most necessary when we think of the witness and service of the church in what I have called 'Galilee'. We need specialist ministries to concentrate on particular structures in our society – industry or education or social responsibility. But if specialist clergy are tempted to do the work themselves instead of regarding themselves strictly as behind-the-scenes enablers of lay men and women, they are just as guilty of paternalism as the old-fashioned, centre-of-the-picture parish priest whom they profess to have supplanted. It is lay men and women who have to discover and follow Christ in Galilee. Priests may also be in Galilee rather than in Jerusalem, but if so, they are there not to tackle the problems themselves, or even to 'tell' the laity how to tackle them, but to help the laity to ask the right questions and consequently to discover for themselves what Christ is calling them to do. Any ordained man or woman who thinks of himself or herself as an expert and tackles the problems directly has ceased to be a pastor; but clergy who understand that their role is to enable Christian people to become more expert and to tackle society's problems with specific reference to their knowledge of Christ are very much pastors.

A good test is to ask what the popular press means when it writes 'church condemns' this or that, or 'church supports' such and such. If it means the clergy or a particular bishop or priest, then we are still failing to be enablers. But when such a statement means that the Christians in a particular place have condemned or supported something, then we can thankfully infer that the clergy there have got the right idea of their function.

So when a parish begins deliberately to organize its life upon a foundation of house-churches and neighbourhood-groups it will not be the job of clergy to lead or preside at the groups but to enable them from behind the scenes by keeping in close touch with those who do lead them, and, if at all possible, convening a regular group consisting of these leaders themselves. Clergy should also be available as resource persons to be called upon when a group has a particular need of their services, either to set out the theological aspects of an issue or to give trained advice on a matter of counselling or of social responsibility, or to fulfil their proper role in an act of worship. But this leads me to the distinctions I believe we must draw afresh between the functions of the different 'orders' of ministry.

The objection which is most frequently raised against the spread of neighbourhood-groups and house-churches is that they too easily become introverted, self-satisfied groups, uninterested in any other gatherings of Christians, and frankly bored by any larger congregational worship because it lacks the intensity which can be experienced in a group of familiar friends. These are perfectly valid observations. But the logical conclusion is not to close down the small groups, but to service them with a ministry that will ensure that each group is made aware of the other groups and of its responsibilities towards them. This calls for a mobile ministry of link-people, not permanently connected to any one group but moving from one to another, just as St Paul moved from church to church around the Mediterranean world, making the church in Corinth aware of the churches of Macedonia, and telling the faithful in the household of Priscilla and Acquila what those in the household of Narcissus were up to. This is the essential apostolic ministry, representing the catholicity of the church to each one of its local manifestations. In the realm of ideas also it means relating the emphasis and enthusiasm of a particular group to the wholeness of Christian doctrine. This is the true *episcopé*, which means not merely administrative oversight but the spiritual gift of 'seeing the whole' and relating each of the parts to the whole. It is a co-ordinating ministry.

Obviously, a great deal of the work of an ordinary incumbent or of a team rector or of a rural dean belongs to this episcopal function. Some thinkers, in fact, advocate actually extending the order of bishops to include these more local episcopal ministries. At some time in the future we may come to recognize and consecrate as bishops those who are exercising this co-ordinating ministry at a variety of administrative levels. In the meantime, one may say, what's in a name? The important thing is for us all to recognize that the primary function of some of the clergy, particularly those in charge of parishes, team ministries or deaneries, is to be the mobile link person and co-ordinator, enabling many different groups of Christians to flourish, and relating them to one another and to the whole.

If the house-group is to be allowed to play its full part in the experience of the individual Christian and in the life of the church as a whole, it must be allowed to possess the fullness of the church as a unit of study, pastoral care, service and witness to the world, and worship. And some of that worship must be sacramental: the church has to be so organized that the eucharist can be celebrated regularly in each of these small groups. At present in the Church of England this immediately means either that the vicar and curates, if there are any, run round from group to group celebrating like 'massing priests'; or, in a more truly New Testament pattern, that an 'elder' is commissioned by authority in the name of the church catholic to preside over the group's meetings, including the celebration of the Lord's Supper.

In all such family groups it is usual that a parent-figure appears with a natural, rather than a professional, gift of pastoral care for the other members. This person is not necessarily the same as the group-leader (to whom I have already referred) but is more likely to be the host of the household. We need to find ways whereby some at least of these natural parent-figures in the different groups can be recognized and ordained to celebrate the sacraments and exercise this basic pastoral care. Once again, let me emphasize, we are a long way from putting this idea into general practice. But I believe we should accept it as the direction towards which each new step that is at present possible to us should be taken. The means most readily available to us at this time is the non-stipendiary priesthood, legally known as the Auxiliary Pastoral Ministry, in which it is possible for a person to be ordained to the priesthood while continuing to earn his or her living in some other walk of life. A careful but deliberate increase in the number of such people, combined with a better enlistment of the help of retired clergy, should make it possible in many parishes for a considerable number of parent-figures of the kind I have described to be properly authorized to celebrate holy communion in house-churches and neighbourhood-groups.

As each neighbourhood-group works out its responsibilities for the healing and building up of its own members, for the drawing in of new ones, and for the service of its local community in a multitude of different ways, it will need to draw upon the expertise of a variety of resource persons. If it feels called to protest against the reluctance of a local landlord to make his empty houses available to the young married couples of the neighbourhood who are still compelled to live with parents, the group will need the expertise of a Christian lawyer. If the group finds itself frequently brought up against pastoral or therapeutic problems it will have to call on a trained counsellor. Such experts may often be found in the secular professions, and it is very important that the church should learn to use the expertise of lay Christians without trying to turn them into clergy. But there is going to be an increasing need for the help of people who, as well as being competent sociologists or counsellors, lawyers or educationalists, are also thoroughly trained to think theologically. So, inevitably as it seems to me, the church will have to recognize a body of professionals on its own pay-roll whose function it is to offer specialist advice and training in one field or another so as to enable ordinary Christians to make a more effective witness in the world.

Such people have quite a different function from that of the episcopal co-ordinator or the parent-figure priest, yet their vocation to the service of the church is just as valid and just as needed. It is for this group that we need to revive the diaconate as a distinct third order of ministry. As I have outlined them the three functions are quite separate. There is no reason why one should lead into another; and there is no reason why one should be paid more than another. Increments in salary should be determined partly by need and partly by responsibility, but function as such should not enter into it. I hope that in years to come a certain number of new ordinands, having considered the question carefully, will feel that their particular vocation is to be a specialist deacon of the sort I have described and will offer to make that their career with no intention of transferring either to the priestly or to the episcopal function.

There is no need for us to rush our fences. So long as we are moving in the general direction I have tried to indicate, we can move a step at a time. The one really important decision each of us has to take is the decision not to be afraid of change, because the church and its future belongs to our onward-marching God.

33

Wait For It!

T. S. Eliot's much-quoted line might have been written for Advent: 'the faith and the hope and the love are all in the waiting'. For the season of Advent, even more than Lent, combines the 'earnest looking forward' with an almost unbearable sense of delay. In these weeks we are not just waiting for Christmas; we are waiting for the Kingdom. We are waiting for God's promises to come true. We are drawn into the labour-pains of the created universe which longs age after age to be delivered. 'How long, O Lord, how long?'

The readings for the Advent season are full of the tension between the expectation of imminent fulfilment and the readiness for a long wait. 'Hold your heads high, because your liberation is near.' 'It is far on in the night, day is near.' 'Blessed is he that comes in the name of the Lord.' 'The Lord is at hand!' But they also speak of the steadiness of stewards who stay at their posts however long the Lord delays, and of the encouragement given by the scriptures so that we may maintain our hope with fortitude. They remind us also of the 10 girls who waited with their lamps lit to be the bridegroom's escort and whose only difference was that half of them were ready for a long wait and half were not.

Every Christian has to learn to live in this tension, strung between the fulfilment and the postponement of the promises of God, strung between 'now' and 'not yet'. We are meant to experience the changed life, for now is the day of salvation. The resurrection of Jesus and the gift of the Spirit really did introduce the new age, the new creation, and the church should be demonstrating this in sicknesses healed and evil overcome and relationships changed and communities shaped by the love of God. And yet – and yet – all this finished work of Christ is accompanied by incompleteness. 'I have *not yet* reached perfection, but I press on, hoping...' 'We do not yet see all things in subjection to man. But we see Jesus...' 'Here and now, dear friends, we are God's children; what we

147

shall be has *not yet* been disclosed.' 'The end is *not yet.*' True salvation, therefore, consists of grasping the beginnings of the new life, the first fruits, which we have already been given, and then enduring in patient hope until the time of the full harvest has come. And it is not for us to judge when that is likely to be.

It is difficult to live in this in-between time, especially when it goes on century after century. To carry on as though a great deal has taken place when most of the evidence shows that nothing has changed makes us look pretty stupid. The embarrassment of it tempts us to relax the tension by coming down wholly on one side or the other.

Parts of the church settle for mediocrity and give up all claim that the coming of Christ has made any visible difference to the world. Christianity of that kind will go on producing a respectable morality, some peace of mind, a tradition of public worship for those who want it, and a decent level of kindness and unselfishness, and to that extent it will be neither better nor worse than any other major religion. But there will be no note of victory nor of miracle nor of anything new under the sun for our threatened race.

Other parts of the church go the other way and settle for impatience. They deny the 'not yet' element in the gospel. They assert that the cross and the resurrection and, even more, the gift of the Spirit, has made the life of heaven available here and now to anyone who will believe it and receive it. Every sin, sickness and setback is to be met by an immediate supernatural intervention. There are even some who go so far as to promise success in worldly affairs by the same miraculous means. And, since these things clearly do not happen on every occasion, all kinds of explanation are advanced to sustain the pretention – lack of faith or secret sin has crept in, or the devil is having a field day.

It is true we do not often see either of these deviations in its extreme form. But there are many who fall into some degree of exaggeration, towards either low-level complacency or impatient fantasy.

I have every sympathy with those who grow dissatisfied with a church that does not really expect God to make a difference to anything at all. It is a wonderful thing when a congregation begins to pray expectantly and finds that prayers are answered. It is great to see such a congregation believing once more that God will speak to them as they worship him, that lives *can* be changed and human situations put right. But they should beware of over-simplifying their story, or they will certainly put people off and end up as a sort of sect, dividing Christians against each other.

Reality is much more likely to be something like this.

Together you will find that God does answer your prayers, but not every time, for it is your unanswered prayers that teach you loyalty.

The gospel you share with others changes some of them, but not all, so that their rejection of it may force you to think it out more honestly.

The Spirit equips you with gifts you did not have before, yet you still fall lest success makes you hard and threatening to others.

You will struggle to bring your local community nearer to God's rule, and you will be frustrated without losing your nerve, for you know his place is with those who wait, not with those who have arrived.

There will be miracles but not too often, for the most precious gift you have to offer others is your weakness.

That is why the Bethlehem story still speaks to the heart of human-kind.

34

The Sense of an Ending

January, as every schoolboy used to know, is named after Janus, the obscure minor Roman god who faces both ways. The bells that ring in the New Year have just tolled the passing of the old one. The end is also the beginning. Our life is a limited number of revolutions. Round and round go the years, faster as time moves on. Round and round go the seasons and the cycles of history, the notable events of our lives, and the small glimmers of personal experience. Round and round rolls the succession of personal crises that leave their scars, of decisions that were difficult to take, of timid arrivals and tearful departures. But do we really learn from the experiences? Do the turning-points give us any change of direction? Round and round go our endless speculations and search for meaning, yet do all our questions lead in the end to the unanswerable, and is time only a treadmill?

> Myself when young did eagerly frequent
> Doctor and Saint, and heard great Argument
> About it and about: but ever more
> Came out by the same Door as in I went.[1]

But that is not the last word. The last word is that eventually, later or sooner than we can imagine, the rhythm of the rise and fall of civilizations, the steady pulse of our world, will, like our own, weaken and cease, and

> The cloud-capped towers, the gorgeous palaces,
> The solemn temples, the great globe itself,
> Yea, all which it inherit, shall dissolve
> And, like this unsubstantial pageant faded,
> Leave not a rack behind.[2]

1. Edward Fitzgerald, *The Rubáiyát of Omar Khayyám*, 1, xxvii.
2. William Shakespeare, *The Tempest*, IV, i.

For around every lovely thing, every moment of value, there hangs the sense of an ending. It lends a poignancy to human life, but it also gives it shape and meaning. In music or in a novel, or a piece of work well done, or a perfect holiday, it is the end and the knowledge that there is going to be an end which gives the whole thing its identity. Limitless future time could have no final aim. With no prospect of arriving, there could be no sense of direction, and all our journeys would be unnecessary.

A good ending is one which makes it possible to see all that has gone before as one integrated whole, to feel that it really is something because it has been something. The end crowns all. But the end may also mar all. So a good ending is even more difficult to achieve than a good beginning.

That is because we have such expectations of the end. We feel it ought to be a perfect climax, and anything that disappoints our anticipation unseats our sense of propriety.

> Like the poet who lived in Japan
> And wrote verses that never would scan,
> When his friends asked him why,
> He would always reply:
> Well, I always try to get as many words into the last line as
> I possibly can.

> But his cousin who lived in Old China
> Said, My verse is very much finer;
> For I always intend
> My last lines to end
> Quite suddenly.

Now, however oddly disturbing the endings of those two limericks may be, they are more true to life than the perfect cadence. Human lives often do end quite suddenly. And civilizations usually die, not with a bang but a whimper, like old men who grow hectic in their retirement and try to get as many words into the last line they possibly can.

Long ago we became suspicious in regard to literature of what Henry James called 'the time-honoured bread sauce of a happy ending'. In fact, we have gone so far in our realism, or is it despair, as to feel that an ending at all is a bad cliché. Perhaps this is why so many recordings of popular songs in these days never die, they simply fade away.

The opening sentence of Jane Austen's *Pride and Prejudice* is renowned as possibly the most perfect beginning to any novel in the English language; but instead of ending with the fine flourish of Elizabeth Bennet's engagement to Mr Darcy, the story runs on into a desultory exchange of letters between the minor characters and a glance at the fortunes of the other sisters. But here, as in her other novels, Jane Austen is more true to life than to high drama. Routine rolls on, and our small personal departures leave only a momentary gap.

At the end of our days few of us can expect to say *Consummatum est* with any great sense of completion. Whether the summons finds us ready or unprepared, we are bound to leave a great deal of unfinished business behind us. That is equally true of the passing of civilizations. However much they have achieved, their collapse is untidy and the relics of their past greatness only make the ensuing chaos seem the more meaningless, while the next wave of cultural energy which will build up into a new era of greatness is still too rudimentary for anyone to recognize the direction from which it is arriving. These inconclusive falls of the curtain do not give us the sense of an ending or gather up the past into a coherent whole. Our instinctive recognition of the natural shape of things tells us that the play is not over. 'The end is not yet.'

The whole of existence is conditioned by those two words: 'not yet'. Every creature, every life-process, every historical development, is doomed to non-fulfilment. We are strung between a sense of progress and an in-built frustration. That is the image St Paul uses to describe the created universe. 'It was made the victim of frustration, not by its own choice, but because of him who made it so; yet always there was hope, because the universe itself is to be freed from the shackles of mortality and enter upon the liberty and splendour of the children of God.' So we live in the light of the promise and under the shadow of the 'not yet'.

But in the midst of this history of non-fulfilment there has been one human life which achieved an ending that made it perfect and complete. Superficially it seemed most terribly cut short and wasted. And yet when he who had lived that life cried *Consummatum est* he was offering up an existence that was total and perfected and all of a piece. That life was terminated not by death alone but by death-and-resurrection, and in it we have seen in anticipation the true ending towards which all things are moving. For him the end was also the beginning, and so it will be for creation itself.

Does it seem strange that the beginning and end of the creation, the beginning and end of time, should be a person? Yet how could it be otherwise? We have all known, in moments of deepest intuition, that our relationship with reality is personal – I and Thou. We have all sensed that the glory and the pain and the mystery of things combine into a single voice that addresses us and demands a reply. These are inklings only, but they make it reasonable to believe that when the end of all things makes sense of the whole, our recognition of the meaning will be like meeting a person, strangely familiar, yet known for the first time.

Bring us, O Lord God, at our last awakening, into the house and gate of heaven, to enter into that gate and dwell in that house, where there shall be no darkness nor dazzling, but one equal light; no noise nor silence, but one equal music; no fears nor hopes, but one equal possession; no ends nor beginnings, but one equal eternity; in the habitations of thy glory and dominion, world without end. Amen.[3]

3. John Donne, adapted from Sermon X in *XXVI Sermons* (1660).

Sources

At the beginning of Parts One, Two and Five are excerpts from three poems, 'Lullaby for the Unsleeping', 'Advent' and 'Under Snow', which were included in *A Christmas Sequence and Other Poems*, published in 1989 by The Amate Press. At the beginning of Part Three are four lines from a poem called 'Love's Self-Opening'; and at the beginning of Part Four is the prayer which John Taylor used as his own daily dedication. This appeared, among other places, in *A Matter of Life and Death*, SCM Press 1986.

The Rosewindow articles were those which John Taylor as Bishop contributed to the *Winchester Churchman*, the monthly journal of the Diocese of Winchester, and are reproduced here by kind permission of the present Bishop of Winchester, the Rt Revd Michael Scott-Joynt. The sermons were preached, as far as I can ascertain, on the following occasions:

1   *In the Beginning*
    New College Chapel, Evensong on 9th Sunday before Christmas,
    29 October 1995

2   *He Could Not Have Come at a Worse Moment*
    Rosewindow 24, December 1976

3   *What Happened*
    Rosewindow 71, December 1980

4   *The True Image of God*
    Winchester Cathedral, Christmas Day 1981

5   *Strangers with Camels*
    Epiphany, 6 January 1988

6   *One Man Stood Up*
    A Second Sermon for Lent

7   *What Shall I Do With Jesus?*
    Farley Mount Open Air Service, Summer 1980; reproduced as
    Rosewindow 69, September 1980